ONE
WAY
BACK

ONE
WAY
BACK

A MEMOIR

CHRISTINE
BLASEY
FORD

ST. MARTIN'S PRESS
NEW YORK

Some names have been changed to protect individuals from further vitriol. Other names have been omitted, including those of my children. However proud I am of them, and they of me, I've chosen to tell my story honestly while avoiding further pain and unwanted attention.

First published in the United States by St. Martin's Press, an imprint of St. Martin's Publishing Group

www.stmartins.com

Excerpt from "We Rise" copyright © 2018 by Amanda Gorman, used with permission of the poet

Frontispiece photo courtesy of Charles Mendler

Photo on dedication page courtesy of Jim Gensheimer

Library of Congress Cataloging-in-Publication Data

Names: Blasey, Christine, author.
Title: One way back : a memoir / Christine Blasey Ford.
Description: New York : St. Martin's Press, 2024.
Identifiers: LCCN 2023051661 | ISBN 9781250289650 (hardcover) | ISBN 9781250289667 (ebook)
Subjects: LCSH: United States. Supreme Court—Officials and employees—Selection and appointment—History—21st century. | Judges—Selection and appointment—United States—History—21st century. | Sexual assault—Law and legislation—United States. | United States. Congress. Senate. Committee on the Judiciary. | Kavanaugh, Brett, 1965– | United States—Politics and government—History—21st century.
Classification: LCC KF8742 .B579 2024 | DDC 347.73/2634—dc23/eng/20231108
LC record available at https://lccn.loc.gov/2023051661

Our books may be purchased in bulk for promotional, educational, or business use. Please contact your local bookseller or the Macmillan Corporate and Premium Sales Department at 1-800-221-7945, extension 5442, or by email at MacmillanSpecialMarkets@macmillan.com.

First Edition: 2024

10 9 8 7 6 5 4 3 2 1

To the letter writers.
Thank you.
I'm finally writing you back.

So we encourage women who dare to stare
Fear square in its face,
Women who've always shown
That when one woman stands up
She is never alone. . . .

. . . .

It is her strength, her story, and her spirit
Which inspires other vital voices
to speak up when they hear it. . . .

. . . .

Here lies, but does not rest, the best
Of tested women who call us all to rise. . . .

—Amanda Gorman, "We Rise," written the
evening of watching Christine Blasey Ford's testimony

CONTENTS

Preface

Most memoirs are the story of a life. This is the life behind a story.

The story happened in the summer and fall of 2018, starting on the beach in the hippie surfer town of Santa Cruz, California, and ending in Washington, DC, with me testifying in front of the Senate Judiciary Committee. Or so I thought.

As a shy person who loathes public speaking, I had tried to avoid going public. As a mom, I had worried about the effects it would have on my children. But as a scientist, I knew I had relevant data that needed to be shared. As a patriotic citizen and someone born and raised on the outskirts of our nation's capital, I saw it as my civic duty, a responsibility to my country to participate in the institutions I had always loved and respected. And as a surfer, I knew I'd already paddled out and there was only one way I was going to get back to shore.

Let me be clear: This is not a political book. Nor is it a manual for victims of sexual assault—there's certainly no handbook that could ever cover what it takes to hold power to account.

I have lessons I learned the hard way, things I wish I'd done differently. I wish I'd known what I needed to do to push the information beyond the closed doors it was kept behind, while maintaining my safety. I wish I had been able to shield my family and friends more from the blowback.

I didn't realize that the testimony would be my only chance to share the data I had.

I wish I'd known there would not be a gradual step into the public eye, one that I could navigate on my own terms. I had lived a relatively quiet life as a mom, professor, and surfer. Quite literally overnight, I became a headline news item. With little preparation, my name would be forever encompassed by one image—me in a navy-blue suit I would never normally wear, being sworn in to solemnly tell the truth. That image told one part of the story. But a more accurate image of the person and the life that had led up to that moment would be me jumping off a rock into the ocean. Just Christine.

I had never even gone by "Christine Blasey Ford." I'd always used Dr. Blasey at work (or simply Blasey to my colleagues), and when I'd gotten married, I haphazardly changed my name to Ford on some things (Social Security) but not others (driver's license). Old friends from back East called me Chrissy. My identity was fractured, dependent on the setting. Suddenly though, it was decided for me. Without signing up for the job but wholeheartedly agreeing with the cause, I was ushered into the #MeToo movement and heralded as a symbol of the importance of believing women, all the while still grappling with my own experience and relation to sexual assault. I didn't take the enormity of the responsibility lightly, nor did I have control over it. It took on a life of its own. One thing was clear: Chrissy was gone. Going forward, I would be known around the world by this three-part label: Christine Blasey Ford.

But I was never really *known*. I was scrutinized, yes. Profiled, sure. Everyone seemed to have an opinion about me. But almost no one knew the real person behind the headlines, the frequently passed-around quote "indelible in the hippocampus."

I'M OFTEN ASKED, "What made you come forward?" like it was a single decision made in one swift move. A swan dive into the stranger-than-fiction political drama surrounding the Supreme Court. In fact, it was more like walking to the diving board, getting to the edge, going back down, and then climbing back up, shifting back and forth, stalling, all the while people watching from the sidelines are alternating between cheers of "Do it!" and screams of "Don't jump!"

People think that I came swinging into the middle of the Supreme Court confirmation hearings at the last minute, an unlikely wrench thrown into a process already steeped in bipartisan messiness. But by my September 27 testimony, I'd been navigating the bureaucratic labyrinth for months. The process of coming forward consisted of a thousand different decisions that happened over the course of the summer of 2018.

Though the methods through which it happened were far from ideal, I never wavered in my belief that sharing this information was essential. If it had been a different job title on the line than Supreme Court justice, perhaps I would have kept quiet. But I just knew I couldn't live with myself if every time the Supreme Court was in the news or made a decision that affected the entire country, I had to think, "I should have said something." I figured at the time that I could lay out the facts and then never have to talk about it again. (Hold for laughs.)

And so I found myself in front of a roomful of senators, lawyers, and reporters, reading a statement I had painstakingly prepared the day before instead of the one that had been written for me. Cameras clicked away. I worried that my voice was too quiet, while also feeling it echo off the walls. It felt as if everyone else in the room was holding their breath. I answered questions that ran the gamut from straightforward to strange. There was no room for nuance, no chance to add any context beyond each carefully worded response.

I was called "the most credible witness in history" by some, but it wasn't because I was a good testifier. My voice was shaking; I was clearly uncomfortable. I think the real reason I was believable was that I had approached it as the scientist I am and taken it as seriously as I did my work. Science is the pursuit of truth, and in that regard, I was a professional.

I couldn't control the outcome—I had divested from that long before I showed up to testify. I could only step up and do what I felt was right, even if I really didn't want to. Once the nomination was confirmed anyway, it was clear that I, and Anita Hill before me, hadn't solved the problem. Unfortunately, many others after us would need to come forward to bring about a larger systemic change. The strange part was that it didn't feel like I hadn't been heard. It felt like I had been believed, but then the response was a proverbial shrug. I couldn't fix the fundamental injustice of that. But I could create a ripple effect by allowing others to hear my story and feel inspired to share theirs.

Of course, I have days when I wish none of it had ever happened. But then I think about the letter writers.

Months after I testified, I finally picked up the mail from my office. I received over a hundred thousand pieces of mail—not emails or text messages but physical letters—in the aftermath of that testimony. There were mountains of them. The statistician that I am, I started classifying them: They came from forty-two different countries and all fifty states. About 75 percent of the letters were from people who thanked me and offered general support; 24 percent were from survivors who shared their stories, many times in excruciating detail that never got easier to read, even when they numbered in the thousands; and a small but terrifying 1 or 2 percent contained hate mail and death threats. (If that seems relatively minor compared to the outpouring of support, I will say that what they lacked in quantity they certainly made up for in horrifying, creative quality. Besides, letter writing wasn't the main vehicle for the hostility. You could simply look to social media to even out the love-hate ratio.) As if it were a data sample, I started scribbling on each envelope with identifying tags: "family member," "rape victim," "survivor narrative," "kid poetry." It might have been a strange thing to do, but it was the only way I knew how to make sense of the sheer volume and intensity of the piles and piles of stories.

Statistics did not help, however, when it came to absorbing

the weight of all that trauma. There were letters from little girls who had watched me on TV and thanked me for being brave, while expressing worry that our country had appointed some-one who hurt women to its highest court. There were stories from women in their sixties and seventies who had been raped decades ago and had carried it with them as a shameful secret all these years. Each story held weight beyond what I can de-scribe. Taken collectively, the significance was unfathomable.

In the midst of a worldwide movement of people proclaiming #MeToo, the letters made it clear that despite the new spotlight shone on abuse, the prevalence was on an inconceivable scale. Generations of people had been forced to stay silent. A common refrain repeated throughout those letters was that, despite the final result, I hadn't told my story in vain.

The letters I received from people all over the world even-tually gave even more clarity to my "Why come forward?" predicament. But I never got to thank the people who wrote them. Statistics had helped me quantify them all, but it ulti-mately was useless in helping me respond. I was only able to look at the data and see that the prevalence of sexual assault was so high it was basically at an epidemic level. It seemed to have happened to almost everyone, and while the stories were all different, the effects they had on the letter writers echoed each other again and again.

Many of the writers said that my testimony had helped val-idate the trauma they had experienced and had given them the courage to share their story—often for the first time. I kept hearing Axl Rose singing in "November Rain," "You're not the only one." (I'm a huge fan of Guns N' Roses, Metallica, Pearl Jam, and Soundgarden.) I wondered what it had done to all these letter writers to watch me testify and then see it not change the final decision. I worried in the months—and then years—that followed that if I shrank back into hiding, it would send the wrong message to anyone I had helped, anyone who had been inspired to share their own story despite all the terrifying reasons to stay silent. It was as if I had crawled out of a cave only to walk back in and tell everyone else who was still hiding inside, "Don't go out there; it's not worth it."

Of course, not everyone who tells the truth about their sexual assault is met with the same response that I was. Whatever you do, do not take my story as a cautionary tale with universal application. In my case, it was unfortunately never just about telling the truth; there were larger power structures that made it impossible to be evaluated as a simple assessment of facts. There were puppet masters behind the scenes who were unconcerned with fair process or due diligence, though those phrases were thrown about incessantly. Apparently, I did such a good job of telling the truth that they had to work even harder. At some point on the phone, a person on my PR team attempting to explain all the vitriol said, "You're sort of a symbol now, so the other side has to destroy it."

"All I did was tell the truth, and he still got the job," I said. "Why are they destroying me?"

"They're destroying *a symbol* of you," she corrected me, as if it were any consolation. "Because a symbol is too important, too unifying, too dangerous."

"Well, the real me is not exactly flourishing," I replied. "The real me is pretty destroyed too." Everyone told me what a good job I had done. But now it felt like I had a target on my back that would never go away.

That's when another PR person said, "You can never be anything else now. You can never be different than you were on that day."

It felt like a sentencing.

I always wonder, if I'd never listened to that and had just gone about my life a little more freely in the aftermath of my testimony, would I be better off now? I suppose this book is my way of breaking free.

IF YOU HAD asked me a couple of years ago why I wanted to write a book, I would have said I wanted to destroy the people behind the political machine that ruined my life. Clearly, I wasn't ready to tell this story.

Now, more than five years out from the testimony, I know you can't write a book based on vendettas. I also know that no one wants a catalog of everything that's ever happened to me. But my story can't just be about the three months in 2018 when my life exploded in front of the world's eyes. My life weaves together surfing, statistics, motherhood, friendship, and politics.

The tricky thing is, I'm used to scientific writing where I stay invisible on the page. I've coauthored numerous papers related to anxiety and trauma; now I'm examining my own, and it's a whole different ball game. I can find correlations among a set of data, but now I'm seeing the patterns in my childhood, in my personal and professional life. It turns out, a PhD dissertation has nothing on a memoir.

Throughout writing this book, I've thought about the opening lines from my testimony: "I am here today not because I want to be. I am terrified. I am here because I believe it is my civic duty to tell you what happened to me."

It applies today. Stepping back into the spotlight comes with an infinite number of things to worry about. Anything I write might be taken out of context or spun to drum up scandal.

I want to help others, but I'm anxious and scared. I think about the letter writers. I think about the death threats. But I keep writing because the whole story hasn't been told. Everyone keeps getting it wrong. There are so many unanswered questions. Why is sexual assault so prevalent, with stigma carried by the victims instead of the perpetrators, and how can we turn that tide?

I'm not just answering these questions for myself. I'm also hoping to answer them for the young women who continue to navigate a patriarchal world where history repeats itself. And for the young boys, including my two sons, who hold so much power and potential to undo the injustice. For the most part, though, this book isn't about what I want people to do. It's about what I want them to understand.

People say to me all the time, "I could never do what you did." And I say, "You don't know until you're thrust into a situation how you'll handle it." Perhaps if I had known just how terrible and long-lasting the consequences would be, I would have chickened out and moved to Costa Rica. The question of why I came forward brings up wild contradictions.

Do I regret it? In many ways, yes.

Would I do it again? Absolutely.

PART
ONE

Santa Cruz

On June 27, 2018, I was sitting on the beach. I had been there all day every day for two and a half weeks while my twelve- and fifteen-year-old sons took part in the Santa Cruz Junior Lifeguard Program, as they'd done every summer since they were six years old. The smell of seaweed and sunscreen cut through the crisp Northern California air. I felt more at home there than perhaps anywhere else in the world. I'd dyed the underside of my hair blue (an annual summer ritual that signified me being out of the office and off duty from my teaching job) and had fully settled into the slow pace of beach life, the layers of my blonde hair ending in cascading blue waves for good measure.

My main responsibility that summer was loading the surfboards, wet suits, and tent into the car and packing the cooler each day with enough supplies to keep myself and two young boys from getting hungry and cranky. My husband, Russell, had a job that wasn't as flexible as mine, so he spent far less time in Santa Cruz. He loves to surf too and joined us on the weekends.

I'd been obsessively following the status of the boys in Thailand who had been stuck in a cave with their soccer coach.

I usually tuned out the news during the summer—we didn't even have cable on the big old TV at our beach house—but I couldn't help checking for an update on the boys' situation. Among the various headlines, one caught my eye: "Anthony Kennedy Retiring from the Supreme Court." "Hmmm," I thought. "I'll need to read more about that later."

That night, I skimmed as many articles as I could find, seeing a name that I'd tried to forget for decades pop up repeatedly. Pundits said he was the likely successor since he was Kennedy's clerk. But it all seemed to be speculation at that point. "Surely it won't be him," I told myself.

Within two days, I started seeing his name mentioned more and more in predictions of who would be nominated. I decided to mention it to my friends Kirsten and Jim, who spent most days on the beach with me as our kids did their Junior Lifeguard activities.

Kirsten is an accountant and the mother of four, including triplets. Perhaps she's always been even-keeled, but I imagine that hardly ever being able to keep all her children in view at the same time has forced her into an extraordinary state of maternal Zen. I've never seen her freak out or even look visibly stressed out.

Jim is from Kentucky, but besides a slight drawl, he could easily pass for a native Californian, with a tall, thin athletic build and health-nut habits. He had been my friend for ten years, though we only saw each other in the summer during Junior Lifeguards. While the other parents left immediately after drop-off, we stayed at the beach all day. I stayed because of the ocean (and because in traffic it was about a thirty-minute drive back to our beach house), and Jim stayed because his kid has type 1 diabetes and he needed to check his insulin after exercises like sand running and lengthy cold-water swimming. Jim, Kirsten, and I had forged a casual friendship over the years, chatting about work and kids. I was about to change all that.

"So, Justice Kennedy is retiring from the Supreme Court and I was attacked in high school and now *that guy* might get the job," I blurted out to them. "What are the odds of that!"

I described it like it was simply a case of bad luck: I *happened* to be the person this guy attacked, and now he *happened* to be one of the people in line for one of the most powerful jobs in the country. A lifetime appointment, at that.

Kirsten's facial expression didn't change as she calmly replied, "Oh, wow." And Jim, who had worked as a photographer for the *San Jose Mercury News*, casually told me that if I wanted to talk to someone in the media, he could help.

Despite the nonchalance, I felt like I should probably do, well, something. But what was the protocol? Luckily, Kirsten, Jim, and I had nothing but time on the beach to figure it out. Perhaps it was the kumbaya vibes, sitting barefoot in the sand, but we assumed it could be easily resolved in a discreet and fair way.

"He wouldn't want people to know. We can probably work it out with him without making it a huge deal."

"What if he's nice now? Maybe we should give him the opportunity to prove his true character."

"Should we call him and have him out here?"

"Nuh-uh, you can't go directly to him, at least not without lawyers."

Lawyers? I didn't want to get lawyers involved. After all, I hadn't done anything wrong. Why would I need legal representation? There had to be another way. Jim suggested going to the media.

"Oh no. I don't want to be on TV," I said, shaking my head.

I imagined those news alerts that came on the air with "We interrupt this broadcast . . ." I thought of examples I'd seen of women associated with accusations against powerful men in politics: Gloria Allred's clients, Monica Lewinsky, and, of course, Anita Hill. The almost circus-like drama and publicity surrounding the horrible things that had happened to these women felt cruel and outlandish—and also sounded like a nightmare for a camera-shy person like myself. I could never do it.

As the days passed, I reassured myself with articles predicting that Donald Trump (being Trump) would pick someone more unexpected, perhaps an outsider who didn't even come from a judicial background. In this case at least, I prayed that he'd look beyond the expected choice. I found myself thinking, "Maybe a fresh perspective on the Supreme Court wouldn't be so bad." Between snack and surf breaks, I'd look out at the notoriously shark-infested waters—nicknamed "the buffet zone"—calculating probabilities and coming up with backup plans.

THE LAID-BACK, PHILOSOPHICAL approach my trio had taken on the beach was short lived. Suddenly we went from feeling like we had all the time in the world to sensing a quickly approaching deadline, the clock ticking toward Trump's scheduled announcement on July 9. I figured that if this was a high-stakes gamble, I couldn't throw in my chips after the game had already started. I thought I could save Trump the embarrassment of choosing an unviable candidate. Maybe he would even thank me for my help? It seems laughable now, but in those early days, it felt like a simple matter of sharing relevant information.

But on a deeper level, there was also a strange moral quandary I was wrestling with. After all, I wasn't a perfect person either. Did I really have the right to say something? Kirsten and I sat around for an entire day and told each other all the bad things we'd ever done.

"I've done cocaine."

"I've done mushrooms."

"I hooked up with this guy, and I don't even remember his name!"

Jim sat there listening to Kirsten and me, quiet and non-judgmental.

"Okay, Jim, your turn," we said.

"I guess there was a time in high school," he replied as we listened eagerly. "This popular guy, kind of a bully, told me to say something mean to this poor kid who didn't really have any friends. I didn't want to say it, but I did. I felt really bad about it. Still do."

This was the worst thing Jim had ever done?

"You can go, Jim. You're dismissed."

We didn't spell out what we were really doing at the time, but it's easy to diagnose in hindsight. The patriarchy was in my blood. I was gaslighting myself before anyone else could do it. Our day of confessions made it clear: I was a flawed person who had done a lot of stupid things. Then Kirsten asked, "But did you ever sexually assault someone?"

She had me there. And Jim asked, "You're the psychologist. Do people change?"

"Yeah," I said. "Some people do."

"Has he changed?"

"I don't know. Maybe."

We concluded that I was not qualified for the Supreme Court. And that I would absolutely have to say something.

I WANTED TO arrange a meeting with a senator, which suddenly brought out the rarely seen Washington insider in me. While I wasn't sure exactly which path I would take, I was familiar enough with that world to know that this kind of tip would likely get fast-tracked to the right people. I believed (hoped?) that I would be able to pass along the information quickly and let them handle it appropriately.

I also knew that people in government didn't work on the weekends (there was that DC insider knowledge again), so I had to say something by Friday, before Trump announced his decision on Monday. More and more articles were predicting he would nominate the ghost from my past, a man I'd tried to forget but who clearly still haunted me. The list had been narrowed down to just him and four others. I read up on the other candidates, begging that they would be picked so I could just let things lie and go on with my life. Meanwhile, my oceanfront sessions with Kirsten and Jim continued, juxtaposing serious conversations huddled together in our beach tents with bodysurfing in the waves. Making calls barefoot with sand crusted around my ankles made it seem like no big deal. But I had a weird feeling. Underneath it all was a percolating sense that it could all blow up at any minute. And then the next moment, a salty spray from a big wave would lightly mist my cheeks and hair, and I'd think, "Oh, no, it'll be fine. Relax."

The Physics of Waves

I've always felt most comfortable in the water. I grew up splashing around in the ocean off Rehoboth Beach, a mid-Atlantic resort town on the Delaware coast, and I swam and dove competitively throughout my childhood and teenage years. When surfing came into my life, it felt like the next logical level of a natural desire to spend all day in the water.

But it was more than that too. Surfing was a welcome escape from the culture I'd grown up in. Being raised in the DC suburbs meant coming of age in a place where country clubs dictated the social scene, where the men talked and the women laughed. I never felt like I quite fit in. When I moved across the country to Southern California for grad school, I felt something that had eluded me my entire life: *I belong here.*

My initiation to surfing was at First Point, an iconic surf break near the Malibu Pier, known for crowds and near-perfect waves. It was nothing short of revelatory. I immediately thought, "I've found my thing." After catching that first wave, I went every day at least once for an entire year. If good waves were expected at 6:00 a.m., I was there. If good waves were expected at 6:00 p.m., I was there. I started sleeping in my car to go out first thing in the morning, before a ton of other people got there. I'd park on the cliff near Leo Carillo State Beach in Malibu, futon mattress stuffed in the back of my tan Jeep Cherokee. My parents would have been horrified, but I knew I was safe because there were other surfers doing the same thing.

There was a lot of riding around in trucks with boys during that time. Just as surfing had been a way to break free from DC culture, the surfers themselves felt wildly different from the boys I'd grown up around. They were two totally different brands of masculinity: the West Coast surfers strong and self-possessed, the East Coast prep school guys performatively misogynistic. Instead of the nervousness I'd always experienced around boys in high school, I felt safe walking into the water with my surfing buddies. They got me.

They also knew where all the good spots were. We'd paddle out, and there would be fifty guys. But where I would have felt intimidated as the only girl at a frat party, being the only girl at a surf spot made me feel cared for. I'd grown up with a forced, formal chivalry, but with the surfers I was the recipient of true gentlemanly behavior, as they let me drop in on waves and let it slide when I inadvertently cut them off. There was a confidence and slight cockiness behind the gestures since they knew they could get any other wave that came along. Might as well give an easy one to the girl, right? It never felt patronizing; it felt like an older sibling giving a younger one the bigger piece of pie. Pure. Honest. Unforced. I loved surfing—and the guys I surfed with—with my entire being.

Every day, when not studying incessantly for my master's in psychology, I paddled out, putting in about a year before I felt like I really knew the scene. I learned by listening to the chatter around me, deciphering quick quips like "That looks like a good break" or "You can't surf at Oxnard Shores; it's heavy local with a steep drop."

However, by the sixth or seventh time you go surfing, you already begin to get a feel for the waves. It starts by knowing the tides. They shift by about forty minutes every day, so you know that if it's low tide at 7:00 a.m. one day, it'll be 7:40ish the next. There are multiple variables at work—in statistics, this is called an interaction effect—so depending on wind speed and duration, some spots work best at mid-tide, while others can be great at high tide. For the most part, though, low tide is key at many surf breaks because when waves come in toward the shore, they have to hit something to break. If there's nothing to stop the energy of the wave—say, the water is too deep—it won't break until it hits the shore. No surf.

The other thing you need for good surf is a swell—a storm, usually thousands of miles away, that sends sets of waves, pushed by the wind, across the ocean. In California, they're coming from either Alaska or the Southern Hemisphere, depending on the season. In the winter, storms coming off the Gulf of Alaska are almost constant, creating daily surf on any part of the coastline facing north from November until March or April.

Nowadays all surf conditions are easily found on the internet. But back in the 1980s and '90s, we just had to watch the waves to scout it out. There were tide calendars too, but part of the fun was going to each spot to check out the tide, see where the waves were breaking. You want to calculate the sweet spot when the waves are best but not too crowded with other surfers. Most of the time, the wind picks up around noon, so you want to go early in the morning or right before dark. Wind is the enemy of surf. It makes the wave crumbly instead of glassy and smooth.

When you're ready, you zip up your wet suit, put the leash around your ankle. You carry your board into the water and wait for a lull in the set. You don't want to paddle right out just to have waves break on top of you. You watch for a little pause in the action, or even a riptide that can help pull you out. This is the hardest part. Sometimes you'll take ten waves on the head, just constant pummeling, until you finally get to a safe spot where you're not going to get pulled back onto shore. You rest for a couple of seconds, take a few breaths. You might have to duck dive under a few more waves, which takes some power. Eventually you turn your board and wait.

How do you decide which wave to take? It's like knowing when to sneeze—it's more about letting it come to you so that by the time it arrives, inertia takes care of the rest. The main thing is to commit. If you try to halfway pull out, you're going to have a worse wipeout than if you had given it your all. So you commit. You start paddling toward the beach as the wave builds behind you. You may have to turn around a little bit to see if you need to speed up or slow down your paddling or adjust your position on the board, but you don't want to overthink it. None of this "Wow, this is a really big wave" or "I don't know if I can do it." You paddle, paddle, paddle and then wait to feel the power of it catch up to you. It's better to pop up too late than too early. If you pop up late, riding most of the wave on your stomach and standing up at the end, you'll still get the wave. That works fine for beginners. But if you pop up too early, you put too much weight on the back of the board. The wave will pass you by.

When you time it right and catch a wave, it's like suddenly having the ability to fly. You're stoked. You don't hear anything, except for maybe a "Whoop!" from another surfer who's psyched for you. Mostly it's the definition of white noise—the ocean literally saying, "Shhhhh."

What you're seeing, on the other hand, is much more chaotic. It's tricky because wherever you look is where your board is going to go, so if you make eye contact with someone, you're probably going to hit them. You want to look at people out of the corner of your eye while focusing on an empty spot in the ocean. It's somewhere between a rush of pure adrenaline and sensory deprivation. You are not of land or air, you are one with the sea, and you don't have the space in your mind to think of anything else.

There's this saying among surfers, "One wave." Meaning that one wave wipes out everything you were worried about before you hit the sand. Renewing your car registration, revising your syllabus, answering emails—all gone. It has a way of transforming fear into a calculated risk, one that you can face with courage or sheer stupidity.

You start with the paddle out, which is often scary, especially on a big day, where a lot of luck is involved in even making it out before a huge wave sends you back to the beach. Once you drop in, though, the fear goes away. Even if you wipe out, as long as you've committed, you might be held down for a bit, but the ocean will push you back up. It's not really scary; it's just tiring. I used to do it on purpose when I was a kid, because the waves on the East Coast are usually only a foot tall. I'd open my eyes and see all the different colors from the sunlight hitting the water and the sand running through the currents. I'd spin and spin, pretending I was in a washing machine. It's oddly beautiful. But not frightening. The paddle out is the scariest part.

Date Night

I never had a problem committing to a big wave, but when it came to relationships, I could never quite commit. Academia gave me an excuse to delay settling down, and no one had come along who made me feel safe enough to take the plunge.

Until I found Russell. We met in the most Silicon Valley way, through an early matchmaking site right around Y2K, while he was a PhD student in mechanical engineering at Stanford and I was a full-time research psychologist in the psychiatry department. I had recently moved from Los Angeles to Mountain View, the future home of Google. At that time, though, in the late nineties, it was just a sleepy town with no nightlife. I was bored, and at least with this dating site I knew I'd meet smart and interesting people, even if it meant that one date consisted of getting a tour of the microchip factory at Intel and most of the dates didn't go further than a cup of coffee.

I went on a *lot* of dates during this time. It was a strange scene, and I found myself once again navigating a new brand of male psyche, different from the buttoned-up but precarious East Coast masculinity and the gentle but rugged SoCal bravado. These Bay Area guys were . . . not exactly effusive. What they lacked in emotional vulnerability, they tended to make up for with dedication to their jobs and passion for intense weekend sports—mostly mountain biking and running marathons.

About fifty dates into my online dating adventure, Russell came up as my number one match, likely because we both had a PhD-level education and were into surfing (I'd matched with plenty of guys who checked both of those boxes, but female PhD surfers were few and far between, so he'd found a needle in a haystack). Each person's profile had answers to questions like, "Who is the one person dead or alive you'd want to have lunch with?" or "What kind of movies do you like?" and as I read Russell's profile, I chuckled over the fact that he'd listed "tearjerkers" as his favorite movie genre. For the question "What are your intentions on this site?" he answered, "Getting married and having children." My response was "Having somebody to surf with." "Who is this guy?" I thought. All the other men on the site were very cavalier, very "looking to meet new people and see how it goes." Meanwhile, this guy was looking for his soulmate to watch sappy movies with? "He's going to get annihilated," I thought. "But he surfs, so let's give it a shot."

On our first date, we went to a restaurant in the yuppie downtown area of nearby Los Altos because he thought there would be live music, but when we showed up, there was no band in sight. We sat down in the quiet restaurant with nothing to break the ice, but it didn't feel as awkward as it had on other first dates I'd been on. The first thing that struck me about Russell was his smile—broad, toothy, charming. I watched him from across the table and realized he had the ability to talk and smile at the same time. "Does everyone do that?" I wondered.

Why had I never noticed it with anyone else? He was respectful and undeniably cute, but he kept bringing up ex-girlfriends, rambling on about how he'd traveled through Mexico with some girl in the past as if that would impress me. Seeing that there was still something genuine underneath the clunky conversation, I chalked it up to him being an engineer. After dinner, I thanked him for a good time and called it a night.

The next day, Russell sent me an email wishing me all the best since it "obviously didn't work out." I was shocked and confused. I had to go and teach a class right after I read it, and I was surprised how rattled I felt and how hard it was to compartmentalize. Maybe that dorky engineer had left more of an impression than I thought? After my class ended, I told my friend Lance—a guy I'd also met on the site but who had ended up strictly a surfing friend—that the guy I'd been on a date with the night before sent me a weird message and that I was dumbfounded because I liked him and thought it had been a perfectly fine first date. Lance told me, "If it's that confusing, you should figure out what the miscommunication was so you know for the next person you date. Just ask him."

I sucked it up and wrote back, telling Russell I'd had fun and was a bit puzzled by his note. He replied immediately. Apparently, he'd thought that if I really liked him, we would've hung out all night. But most of the dates I'd been on up until that point had been twenty-minute coffee meetups. I'd stayed out until 10:00 p.m.! Clearly, we were just playing by different rules. We decided to go surfing for our next date, which was a much better idea.

He picked me up that weekend, and we drove from Santa Cruz to the foggy, coastal cliffs of Pacifica as we traded notes on different surf spots. The weather was superbly shitty. We kept getting out of the car and evaluating the conditions, eventually conceding that good waves were just not happening that day. Despite the weather, it was a perfect date. I hadn't had anyone to do that with since I'd lived in LA. Every weekend, I had driven by myself from Mountain View, over the treacherous Highway 17, up the coast to Half Moon Bay, and over the hill back home. Now I had a companion. I was thirty-five, and he was thirty-nine, both of us at the age where you don't keep dating someone unless you think it's really going somewhere. We've been together ever since.

SEVENTEEN YEARS AND two kids later, on the night before the Fourth of July, we were going on a very different kind of date.

We biked to Riva, a bar and restaurant overlooking Steamers Lane, one of the best surf breaks in Santa Cruz. Most people go for the drinks and the view of the lighthouse and the ocean. I was looking out at the waves, scoping out the surf for the next day. We got our usual order: oysters guacamole and oysters verde, broiled and served with melted cheese on top. Not the most sophisticated way to serve oysters, but incredibly delicious.

"Okay, so I'm going to do it," I announced, my hands unclasping and lying flat on the table as if to add resolution to the news.

"Okay then, let's do it," Russell responded, as if it were as simple as that. Ever the optimist, Russell tended to balance out my overthinking. He was Occam's razor personified—he didn't like getting bogged down in the details and usually drew a straight line to his conclusions. Whereas I could deliberate options endlessly, he preferred picking a plan and executing it. We'd decide to do a weekend trip to San Diego, and I'd ask him if he wanted to see the three hotels I was looking at, to which he'd reply, "Just pick one." I would be playing out every possible situation, and he would say, "I trust you." It was refreshing, and maddening, and quite possibly the key to our success as a couple.

"I need to figure it all out in the next couple days," I continued. "But I'm pretty sure I'm going to tell our Palo Alto representative, Anna Eshoo. A lot of people at Stanford know her, and she's supposed to be really nice."

I kept staring at the water, assessing. There were three or four surf breaks along the coastline. A few surfers were still out there as the sun dipped lower on the horizon. It looked like the south swell was picking up.

"God, Russell, I don't even know what I'm doing," I confessed. "But I guess I'm doing it."

"I'm behind you, baby," Russell said. "We're both in this."

I looked at him, not sure whether I was searching his face for reassurance or permission to abandon the whole thing. I thought about everything we'd been through and how steady a presence he'd always been. He had barely changed since our first date. His hair was a little grayer, his chin had more stubble these days, but his personality had never wavered: optimistic, nonconfrontational, and never one to hold a grudge. We'd had such a short time together, just the two of us, before having kids. We were married on June 21, and I was pregnant by the end of July. Nearly our entire relationship had revolved around raising our sons.

"I need to tell the kids," I said.

Russell's lip curled almost imperceptibly. Neither of us wanted to bring them into this. Ironically, they'd had the best summer ever while I'd been wrapped up in this mess, since it meant I gave them endless quarters for arcade games while I deliberated with Kirsten at the pizza place. They were the personification of "ignorance is bliss." But that bubble would have to burst.

"I'm going to at least tell the older one," I reasoned. "I'll talk to him before I contact the congresswoman."

"Good plan," Russell replied. "Then you can stop stressing about this and enjoy the rest of the summer. You've been worrying about this for what, five days?"

I looked out the window. Had it only been five days? Or thirty-six years?

"You got this, Christine," Russell said. "Just tell her, and then you'll be done."

Independence Day

By the next day, the Fourth of July, my older son was already getting suspicious. He was fifteen at the time, spending his ninth summer in the Junior Lifeguard Program. He was used to seeing me on my board most of the day, shark spotting while he and his buddies learned to be good coastal citizens and keep the beaches safe. He had never seemed to mind that I was always there; I never thought he took much notice of me at all. But it was clear he'd clocked a change in my behavior from afar.

"You and your friends spent the whole time talking by the tent today," he had said to me earlier in the week.

"Oh yeah," I replied casually. "I just never get to see Jim and Kirsten the rest of the year. There's a lot to catch up on."

But he wasn't satisfied. He kept prodding.

"You guys talked a lot again today," he said the following day.

There was an uneasiness to his voice that in turn made me dodgier.

Then: "I kept seeing you walk to your car to make phone calls. Is everything okay?"

I hardly ever use my phone at the beach. Definitely a red flag.

Then: "I saw you put on your wet suit and not go in the water."

Now this was the dead giveaway—the ultimate act of surfing sacrilege—to put on your wet suit and not go in the water. Not my ethos. I needed to tell him what was going on.

Our son was at the point in his surfing development where he didn't need me to go out in the water with him. But I still liked to be at the same break, even if I wasn't close enough to talk to him while we surfed. As I planned how I would explain the situation to him, I decided to let him go out surfing by himself that evening. I figured I'd give him that taste of independence before all of this came crashing down on our family. A kind of last supper before I ruined his life.

We drove to Pleasure Point, an appropriately named surf break on the east side of town, more laid back than the breaks by our house. He threw a shirt over his head as I tried to take a photo of him to capture the moment. I watched him enter the water, his skinny little body in a red wet suit zipping around in the waves, as I sat in my minivan and listened to two songs on repeat, switching between Pearl Jam's "Release" and Bruce Springsteen's "Independence Day." I thought about our son while Eddie Vedder belted out: "I'll ride the wave / Where it takes me / I'll hold the pain / Release me."

Our older son had always been a bit of an outlier in our family, which had made me feel even more of a kinship with him. While my younger son looked a lot like me, with his thick blond hair and happy-go-lucky smile, the older one had darker hair, a delicate face, and a wise understanding that went far beyond his years. He'd been a really sensitive kid who seemed to have a keen awareness of emotions from an early age. Now he was the same age I'd been on that fateful night in high school. I wasn't sure how much he knew about sex (I'd talked to him about the basics, but as he got older, those kinds of conversations became Russell's department), and I worried about casting a dark shadow over the subject before he'd even been exposed to the lighter aspects of teenage romance. Springsteen's song wasn't just appropriate for the holiday; his lyrics seemed to narrate the crossroads we were at: "It's Independence Day / all down the line . . . soon everything we've known will just be swept away."

When we got home, I asked my son to come to my room. As I sat on the bed, his small frame leaned against the doorway (he was always in the tenth percentile as a baby and hadn't had his growth spurt yet). But despite the fact that he still called me Mommy, he seemed more grown up, pleased with his solo session at Pleasure Point. I knew the time had come.

"Hey, kiddo, I know I've been acting kind of strange at the beach," I began. "A lot's going on. You've seen me making phone calls, and I just want to let you know what's happening."

"Okayyyy . . . What?"

"The president is hiring someone for a really important job," I said.

He raised his eyebrows—this was definitely not what he had expected.

"I knew the guy he's thinking about hiring when I was your age. And he did something really bad to me."

"What do you mean?"

I didn't want to tell him the whole story just then. I racked my brain for a way to soften the blow.

"Well, are there kids at your school that do bad things?"

"Oh, *yeah*." He nodded enthusiastically.

"Shit," I thought. "Now I want to know more about that. But let's get through this conversation first."

"Well, this guy was kind of like that. What you're seeing me do on the beach and on my phone is, I'm trying to figure out a way to tell the president that this guy did a really bad thing."

He looked at me, and I held my breath.

"Do you think he'll get the job?" he asked.

"Maybe," I answered. "Either way, it's the right thing to do because it's a really serious job."

He considered for a moment.

"Mommy, that's really nice of you to help the government like that."

He had been taking US history at the time and had gone to DC every year to visit my parents, where he had posed for pictures in front of the Lincoln Memorial, the Emancipation Proclamation, and the Gettysburg Address on our way to the beach or a Nationals game. His response wasn't totally out of left field, but I still found it interesting that his mind went there of all places. I felt a momentary pride that my son, despite being raised nowhere near our nation's capital, had picked up a little of my own sense of patriotism and civic duty. Chip off the old block. I waited for more questions.

"Can I go watch baseball now?" he said.

He didn't ask me anything else about what had happened in high school or why it was suddenly involving the president. He didn't wonder why I wasn't telling his little brother (for better or worse, I thought twelve was too young at the time). He just went about his business until the next night, when he came to my room again.

"Mommy, you know that thing you told me last night? I think I know what it is."

"Oh, you do?"

"Yeah. And I just want to say I'm sorry that happened to you. If you want to talk to me about it, you can. And if you don't, that's okay too."

I don't know what he'd done to try to figure it out. Or maybe he was completely mistaken at the time. But he had given me the kind of response my psychology schooling had trained me to give to people who had gone through something traumatic. "We've done all right with this kid," I thought.

The next moment brought a wave of relief as I realized, "Okay, now I've told him, so when I'm on the phone or talking to Kirsten and Jim or if I have to go to Palo Alto and meet with a representative, at least I won't have to hide it from him."

But another part of me realized that with this step, the pieces were all falling into place. Russell was on board. Our older son was in the loop. Our younger son was going to have a slower rollout, but we'd deal with that. Now it was time for action. Tomorrow I'd make the call.

Beltway Baby

If only it were that simple. Calling a senator, much less the powers that controlled the Senate Judiciary Committee, would force me to step back into a world I had left years earlier. I had chosen a life on the West Coast among the waves. But I had originally come from a place of imposing halls, hushed voices, the sanctity of bureaucratic formality, and long-standing tradition.

I had grown up just outside the Beltway, the metropolitan area surrounding Washington, DC. It was like growing up in Hollywood in a way. While Hollywood revolves around show business, "inside the Beltway" is shorthand for the business of politics, which infuses just about every aspect of daily life. In both cases, the insulated environment you inhabit becomes the center of the universe, the place where anything that's important is happening.

We all lived in colonial houses, with their neat, symmetrical predictability. Anytime I've gone back and driven through the streets, especially with people who didn't grow up there, it's felt like driving through a sea of bricks. But there's a grandeur to the area, where national monuments are as common as movie theaters, with no high-rises to compete with the Capitol dome or the Washington Monument. It's like living inside the country's trophy case. We're a relatively young nation, but you can feel the history seeping through every vein of the city. It's undeniably impressive, and the beauty of the architecture never loses its majesty. The Lincoln Memorial, the Vietnam Memorial—I could visit them every week, and it would still be breathtaking. It's the equivalent of seeing a whale in the ocean. I'm never over it. It's never not cool.

There was a certain power that came with living there, even if it was in reality just an upscale district surrounded by a circular freeway. There was a sense, especially in the seventies and eighties, when America was seen as the preeminent world power, that we lived in the most important place in the most important country in the world—as fraught and misguided as that attitude may have been. The fact that the area was an actual circle gave it even more of an exclusivity, as if it were the nucleus at the core of this global, commanding force around which everything else orbited. We were sometimes told that if someone were to hit the United States with a nuclear bomb, they would target DC, as if that were something to be proud of. And yet we were proud because that was the culture we had grown up in.

My family was casually Protestant, and I went to public school until sixth grade, but the religion I was taught at school was Government with a capital *G*. Our field trips were not to the aquarium but to Arlington Cemetery, Mount Vernon, and the theater where Lincoln was shot. We had mock elections and studied how the legislature worked. All of my classmates could have swept a "Government" category in *Jeopardy* in our sleep.

The very first overtly political thing I remember was when I was around six years old. A school bus drove by, and in one of the windows, a kid not much older than me held up a cardboard sign that read "Impeach Nixon." I didn't even know what it meant (perhaps something to do with the president and peaches?), but it stopped me in my tracks.

Neither of my parents were actively involved in politics, but I remember them being upset when Jimmy Carter got elected and absorbing from their reaction that something *really bad* had happened (taxes would go up, and Big Government would take over). In our community, having a friend whose parent worked in politics was as mundane as it was glamorous. President Ford's daughter had gone to my school a few years before me, and many of my schoolmates had parents who were senators.

Most families I knew were Republican, which certainly didn't have the same meaning then as it does today. Back then, the party was primarily socially moderate, pro-business, and, of course, not big on taxes. It was about supporting traditional values and a low level of government interference.

It wasn't even so much a conscious choice to be Republican there; it was simply the norm. Our parents were, so their kids were too, simple as that. My friends and I thought Republicans were the ones who balanced the budget and kept us safe from wars. Who would object to that? We all joined the Young Republicans, not because we wanted to make a political statement but because it was just another club to belong to, like being in the Girl Scouts. If anything, the main draw was getting the little elephant pin you could wear on the collar of your turtleneck sweater. Or getting to go to the Republican Convention (I always wanted to go but was never invited).

It's important for me to point out here that I don't think negatively about the Republican Party, which is a confusing and seemingly contradictory statement for most people to hear considering how it ended up affecting my life. What was cause for concern was the way a one-sided culture was allowed to homogenize and fester.

Living in the Beltway area, we all absorbed our parents' ideologies simply because we weren't exposed to any others. I didn't give much thought to the fact that we lived in a two-party country because I only really saw one of them. It wasn't until I moved to California in my early twenties that I realized we had been secluded within a web of private schools and country clubs, with a correspondingly myopic outlook.

It was a strange discovery because I hadn't been sheltered, per se. It wasn't as if I had grown up on some rural farm, miles from other people. In fact, it was the opposite. Everyone knew everyone—or at least knew their cousin or their uncle. Information and access were easily passed along. Everyone hired everyone else's kids. It was a well-established network, more of an institution than isolation. I may have been in a bubble, but I was in good company, for the most part.

That's why people who are from the place I'm from mostly stay. I, on the other hand, left that incubator community and its facade of safety and security. I didn't realize that leaving meant eventually I'd never be able to come back.

Every Wave Starts with a Ripple

In graduate school, I studied marriage and family therapy, including the work of fellow Stanford alum Jay Haley, a disruptive pioneer in psychology and author of the book *Leaving Home*. I loved his strategic family therapy approach, developed at the Mental Research Institute in Palo Alto, which used creative techniques that defied earlier approaches where the therapist sat back and let the client lead the session. Instead, Haley's methods often challenged the clients with unique instructions and interactions, combined with a careful review of the results and ongoing experimentation.

Within the families Haley worked with, there would be the "identified patient," a term coined by anthropologist Gregory Bateson referring to the person who had essentially brought the family in for therapy in the first place. It could be for mental health problems, substance abuse, behavior issues, or other reasons. But the problems discussed in therapy would not be exclusive to that identified patient. In fact, Haley would look at those issues as attempts to cope with other situations happening within the family unit. He would identify which problems could potentially be solved, set metrics for success, and design interventions. Instead of just looking at the identified patient's depression as anger turned inward, he would examine it as one piece of the larger family dynamic.

Family therapy, or "systems theory," likened the family unit to one of those mobiles you hang above a baby's crib. Each person in the family is linked together, so if one piece moves and disrupts the balance, all the others get tangled up as well. It's not one individual creating the chaos; it's the entire family unit as a whole. Haley prescribed interventions that would further disrupt the mobile, recommending that the identified patient do *more* drugs or that the family members temporarily refrain from the efforts they'd been making, allowing them to then proactively swing the pendulum from resisting change to actively desiring change.

Clearly, this was pretty rock and roll. I devoured everything I could read about it.

I suppose I had a special interest. I am the identified patient in my family. The disruptor. I guess I always have been.

My DAD WAS the most formative influence on my childhood, my hero really, and I think he deserved every bit of adulation I bestowed upon him. Unlike almost everyone else in our community, he had not come from money. Quite the opposite. He was an only child from Silver Spring, a more racially diverse (though heavily segregated) and working-class area. He got in a decent amount of trouble in his youth before joining the military and turning his life around. He met and married my mom when they were just twenty, and they quickly got to work on their nuclear family, having me and my two older brothers within six years.

My dad has always been well-dressed and charismatic. He is as friendly as he is imposing. Despite running in social circles where he often had less formal education than his peers, he's always been regarded as smart and popular. He knew just how far to take the fun before it got him in trouble. He ran a tight ship at home, raising us almost as if we were in the military, but he also woke us up some mornings belting Nat King Cole's "Mona Lisa." Every Christmas, we would gather around to watch *Patton*, a revered annual tradition, after opening presents and personalized stockings my mom needlepointed by hand.

My dad was always incredibly involved in our lives, and he taught us practical life skills and street smarts, like how to buy a car without getting worked over by the salesperson. He wanted his kids to have everything he hadn't had in his own life, and he'd do anything to make that happen.

My mom and dad balanced each other well, with my mom's mild-mannered, conciliatory demeanor neutralizing my dad's gregarious, strong-willed energy. My mom was cooperative, agreeable, understanding. She was a classic stay-at-home mother, happily stationed in her role as a suburban wife. I don't think she ever saw her life as self-sacrificing, but she'd often tell my brothers and me, "I love you guys more than I love myself."

When I was in kindergarten, we moved from Silver Spring to Potomac after someone got shot at the nearby Safeway. That was all it took for my dad to pick up and go.

Potomac was a much nicer town. My parents had a house built in one of those neighborhoods where every five houses look exactly the same. But a lot of my friends and classmates lived in the pricey area, so in comparison I assumed we were poor. I guess when you're surrounded by an abundance of outrageous wealth, your standards get skewed. It's all relative to what you see.

Despite feeling slightly different from my peers, I had a happy childhood along with my two brothers, Ralph and Tom. Ralph was born six years before me, so he was always in a different school and friend group. I saw Ralph as the golden child—a popular star quarterback, everyone's favorite. Tom was born only eighteen months before me and was drastically different from Ralph, more introverted. Like many families, there were good times mixed with a dose of sibling rivalry in our house growing up. They were typical older brothers, and I was easy pickings as the youngest and most sensitive.

But for much of my early years, I spent most of my time in my room, with the door closed, listening to Casey Kasem's *American Top 40* countdown show while lying on my pink canopy bed, thinking, "I'm in the wrong family." The music helped drown out the nagging question of whether I was the crazy one or they were. In either case, there was a mismatch, and I knew I needed to figure a way out of my situation.

AT THE TIME, I didn't know that education would prove to be my escape route. My dad had always been so singularly focused on school. He had gone to the public Montgomery Blair High School in Silver Spring and, after his time in the military, to a trade-level banking school at Northwestern, but he never received a college degree. My mom had gone to secretarial school and taken some college classes but never finished. They were both determined for their kids to get the education they hadn't—or at least my mom was on board with my dad's obsession with it. He believed it was the ticket to everything, and still does. And in his mind, private schools were the best shot at top-level schooling. He was committed to doing whatever it took to get us in.

My dad started his own business, leasing computers and office furniture to companies. He worked tirelessly, sometimes having to travel out of state to make a sale, despite a fear of flying, which he unsuccessfully tried to conceal, showing unmistakable stress and irritability in the lead-up to any trip.

I was in seventh grade when he was finally able to put me in private school, at Holton-Arms, an all-girls prep school in Bethesda. My brother Tom went to Landon, Holton's brother school, while my oldest brother, Ralph, went off to college.

While it was a huge achievement for my dad, it was a tough transition for me. Holton-Arms was a school for kids whose parents were ambassadors and VIPs—the princesses of Jordan went there, driving up to school in a limousine, accompanied by bodyguards.

The high-profile student body meant that the academic standards were considerably higher than in the public schools. Before the school year even started, I had been assigned to read *The Once and Future King*, about the legend of King Arthur. It seemed a strange introduction to an all-female school, to be reading all about men, but I shrugged and tried to memorize what each (male) character did. When we finally read more modern books, I was captivated by *The Great Gatsby* because it reminded me of the people who surrounded me. It opened a tiny door for me with the realization that one could look upon these fancy people with a critical eye.

I'd begun to feel like an outsider at an early age, and the move to private school turned it up a notch. All of a sudden, I was in school with kids who had known each other since third grade. My parents kept telling me how lucky I was, but all I felt was lonely.

And awkward. It's hard to pinpoint how much of my angst could be attributed to the school switch and how much could be chalked up to the fact that I was twelve and that the experience seems fairly universal in its uncomfortable agony. I desperately wanted to fit in, and even though I felt embarrassed in my own body, I was naturally cheerful and easy to get along with. I made friends quickly and started getting invited to after-school get-togethers.

But my parents were also very strict with me. I had serious rules about where I could and couldn't go. I wasn't allowed to walk outside of the development we lived in, much less navigate crosstown trips to hang out with my new friends. My mom was afraid of the unknown and offered vague warnings that "there's people out there that will do stuff." I would shake it off and go right ahead, wandering beyond my limits. I'd walk through the big cement sewer tunnels, imagining I was in a Nancy Drew novel. The only thing I was scared of was my parents finding out. When my mom inevitably found out through word of mouth or my obvious absence from the pool, swing set, and trampoline, she would be furious. She told me I could have been drowned by water coming through the pipes. Just like the Safeway shooting that had prompted our move from Silver Spring, these clear and present dangers spooked her. Neither she nor my dad imagined any harm would come from the private school world they had worked so hard to get me into.

As THE LATE seventies gave way to the early eighties, preppy culture took over, and already being prep school kids, we doubled down on it. All the girls wore pink-and-green Fair Isle sweaters and wide-wale corduroys with ribbon belts. The sleeves were puffy, and the hair was feathered. My mom loved taking me shopping, and while I didn't really enjoy it, I liked having something that brought us together, the two supporting females in a male-centric family.

Of course, at school we had to wear a uniform: a navy-blue sweater, white button-down blouse, and green-and-navy plaid skirt, which we could not alter in any way. Some girls tried to hem theirs ever so slightly shorter, but I didn't have the sewing skills or the desire. Besides, the girls who modified their uniforms always got caught.

I may not have gotten dress code violations, but I found plenty of other ways to get in trouble. I'd always been the most difficult sibling at home, but now I also began talking back to teachers. My parents had developed a different set of rules for me than for my brothers, and I had already gotten used to being singled out for discipline and thus rebelled against it even more. I'm sure part of it was just the age-old protectiveness over young girls and the freedom given to young boys, but if I'm being honest, my brothers were also more responsible, more trustworthy. I can't blame my parents for being stricter with me. Nevertheless, there was also a sort of chicken-or-egg thing—I wasn't sure if I had more rules because I violated them more

or if they cracked down on me more and I violated the rules
as a result. Regardless, once the dynamic was set into motion,
our family unit, our mobile, if you will, had established itself:
My brothers were allowed to do almost anything they wanted,
while my limits were set in stone. My curfew was much earlier
than that of my brother who was in the same grade as I was.
Even our chores were assigned unevenly, with me doing the
dishes (365 days a year) and my brothers sharing the job of
mowing the lawn (only in the summer and, even then, only
once a week or so).

I don't fault my parents in the least—there was a baked-in
separation between genders that permeated all the families we
knew, including our own extended family. Every Thanksgiving
or Christmas, the women in my family would be in the kitchen
chatting, cooking, and cleaning while the men watched football in another room. It wasn't as if women were banished—the
kitchen was also where all the fun was, where we could be near
Maw and listen to all the family stories.

Living in the land of our founding fathers, built on a system
of power that was created by and for men, of course men and
women were treated differently and kept conveniently separate.
So the boys went to all-boys schools, where they could look up
to men, and the girls went to all-girls schools, where they could
also look up to men. We had coed teachers, but the male teachers were our favorites. I remember one female English teacher
who in hindsight was clearly a feminist, but she certainly didn't
publicly identify as such.

The boys in the neighboring private schools would be held
back if they were having trouble in class, but the girls wouldn't,
so by senior year we'd be dating the sophomore boys because

they were closer to our age. It ruffled the feathers of the boys' moms, but not more so than if their sons hadn't had the chance for a redo, ensuring their records kept them on the path to high-powered positions. Meanwhile, though the expectation for the girls was 100 percent college matriculation, no one was trying to get us on the fast track to any sort of career. The main directives were to do well in class, behave nicely, and be respectful.

We were all just products of the time and place we were living in.

We did as we were told. It wasn't until I was in college that I really had any conversations about feminism.

When I was a teenage girl, my main concern was, "Am I going to be able to go to that party on Friday?" For better or, more realistically, for worse, that was where my energy was going.

The Price of Popularity

I was already the baby in my family, and on top of that, I was younger than everyone else in my class. When I switched from public school to Holton-Arms, the initial culture shock made me feel even more childish. The girls were a lot bolder, much more confident and polished. I was slightly shocked, but it was also strangely attractive. I had previously only been able to entertain the risk taker inside me when diving at the pool. Now there was an outlet for it that also came with the acceptance I craved. Becoming popular was my main priority.

This required a delicate balance, walking a tightrope between my naturally smart and independent nature and the role of an easygoing follower who went with the flow of the crowd. I was a careful troublemaker, going to the park with a friend and sharing one beer we'd swiped from the fridge or surreptitiously smoking a Marlboro Light (we tried cloves, but the smell was too hard to hide). Mostly, I just wanted to get out of the house. And, of course, hang out with boys.

My brother Tom and I had a Venn diagram of overlapping

friends, though he was more reserved than I was, preferring a night at the movies to my usual party scene. He grumbled when I wanted him to drive me to a party, especially because my earlier curfew meant he would have to cut his own night short to get me home on time. He drew the line at me dating any of his friends, whatever that even meant at that age. Most "couples" got together through inertia and spent a few weeks being publicly attached while privately clueless—though one thing was clear: the boy would take charge of any kissing or fooling around that happened, and the girl would follow his lead. We sometimes ventured beyond the pool of Landon boys to hang out with guys from other private schools but never those from public schools.

I would sometimes ask my neighbors what was going on at public school, and it sounded like *Fast Times at Ridgemont High*. I was jealous. They were free. We prep school kids all dressed similarly and behaved similarly. No one was allowed to be outrageous or march to the beat of their own drum. I'd hear stories of the public school parties, which were probably exaggerated but which nevertheless sounded incredibly wild. But then the next thing we knew, the private school kids started having their own parties and went even harder to make up for being late to the (literal) party.

By ninth grade, alcohol started showing up at almost every gathering. My parents didn't let me go out that much, so my experimentation was limited, but I tried beer here and there. Then in tenth grade, as my friends got older and more people got their driver's licenses, there was some additional freedom. Parties happened every weekend. No one wanted to miss anything.

This was the height of an early-eighties John Hughes era that glamorized a hypersexualized, debauched high school party scene as depicted in movies like *The Breakfast Club* and *Sixteen Candles*, where teenage boys were singularly focused on getting drunk and getting laid. The "boys will be boys" rationale was stretched to its limit, even romanticized. Alcohol was a free ticket to exemption from the rules we all lived by and desperately wanted to buck, especially for the guys.

These parties were where the strict standards that had been placed on us academically and reputation-wise were temporarily loosened up. There would be levels of revelry, ranging from people casually sipping beers to some clusters of swaying, animated kids feeling suddenly emboldened, and those few who were obviously, uncontrollably wasted. Even if you were fairly drunk yourself, the people at the end of the spectrum were on a whole other level. Ninety-nine percent of the time, they were male. Every so often, it would be a girl who got really drunk, but it was more of a one-off slipup, a situation they wouldn't get themselves in again because it wasn't acceptable. However, when boys got that drunk, you largely just gave them some space and stayed away, not because they seemed unsafe but because they were generally really annoying. The first few times I saw someone that messed up, I felt mortified on their behalf. "God," I thought, "they're going to regret this tomorrow." But then the next time we saw them they'd be laughing about their antics, no harm done. There was never a sense—at least before the summer of my sophomore year—that drunk guys were something to be afraid of. We just awkwardly laughed as they made fools of themselves.

My parents never really talked to me about parties and alcohol. The only thing they told me was to be home by eleven thirty or I'd never go out again. They always had to know who was having the party, who was going, and whether parents were going to be home, but the only follow-up they ever made was asking me the next morning whether I'd said hello to the mother and father and thanked them for having me over.

If my parents hadn't sat me down to talk about parties and alcohol, they most certainly didn't touch the sex conversation with a ten-foot pole. My mom used her usual well-meaning scare tactics to warn me about boys, telling me after she saw me talking to a lifeguard I knew at the pool, "Chrissy, you are fourteen and he is sixteen, and you need to know that sixteen-year-old boys only want one thing from you. And it's not to be your friend." To be fair, no one I knew learned about sex or gender dynamics from their parents, and my own did the best they could. One day my mom handed me the *Encyclopedia of Adolescence*, a series that came in a three-book box set that described how teenage brains and bodies change. I read them, but they weren't necessarily sufficient. There was definitely nothing about consent. The closest I got was coded language passed around school about which boys to hang out with and which ones to avoid, but the qualifications were mostly about which country club they belonged to. I had no reason to be suspicious of boys. I just wanted to be friends with them.

One night, I ended up at a gathering with my girlfriend Leland and a couple of guys from Georgetown Prep, Landon's rival school.

I've already publicly described in detail what happened to me during that party when I went upstairs to use the bathroom. The transcriptions of it reside in the annals of our judicial records or just beyond an easy Google search for anyone interested. For several decades, I kept the events of that night a secret.

As an adult, I would finally explore the full depth of its effect on me and my life. But as a fifteen-year-old whose top priorities were being invited to parties and avoiding trouble with my parents, I told myself when I got home that evening that the night had been a success. I had gone to a party, I'd made it out of that house when things went awry, and I had gotten home before curfew without my parents knowing what had happened. As terrifying as it had been, it also had seemed normal. Not right, but not rare.

That night, I lay down in bed and felt more worried about what the others at the party might think of me than about the fact that I'd experienced an assault that would alter the course of my life and come back to haunt me decades later. "They're not going to invite me to their parties anymore," I thought. I felt both disappointed and relieved.

How DID I end up at that party in the summer of 1982? There has been so much emphasis on the literal how—who drove me there, how I knew the boys. But the larger answer to the question is far more interesting. How did I end up being a girl who went to parties with boys she didn't really know? Someone who drank beer and lied to her parents? I'll never know exactly what path led me to that night, but I do know that the question of why I went to parties became easier to answer afterward. Before that night, I went to belong. After that night, I went to escape.

Indelible

Is that night the reason I have anxiety? The reason I don't like being in small, enclosed spaces? The reason I went from being an obnoxious pupil who constantly interrupted class to a quiet introvert with self-esteem issues? The reason I became self-destructive in the years that followed?

People want to draw a clear, straight line from a singular experience to an end result. They want to say *x* causes *y*; case dismissed. But that's a flawed conclusion. Correlation is not causation. What I experienced is just one expression of the entirety of my life. If my life were a graph of traumatic factors, that night would be a spike on the axis, but it's all wrapped up in a pretty complex picture.

There's a concept in psychology called the "unthought known," coined in the eighties by psychoanalyst Christopher Bollas (a couple of decades later, it would also become the name of a very underrated Pearl Jam song), which describes an experience that is subconsciously known but not thought about or remembered in a deliberate way. Often something traumatic, the unthought known, once experienced, is pushed down, shunned from our everyday thought processes. However, it doesn't go away completely. It sets up shop deep within us, influencing our behavior without us ever having to remind ourselves of what happened.

I didn't consciously think much about my sexual assault after it had happened. I shut the door on it and filed it away like any other memory. Decades later, I was forced to uncover it and bring it back into the light, not because I had intentionally blocked it but because it was like anything else you don't think of on an everyday basis. The same way that if you asked me to recall something from kindergarten, I could pull a memory up, but it's not top of mind.

My memory was picked apart on a worldwide stage by neuroscience experts and talking heads in 2018 and the years that followed. But I welcome anyone to pick a random night out of their high school years and try to recall every single detail of it. Like anything else, the things you think about most are the things that survive and take on more life with the years. Certain things get washed away with time, while others become more distinct with the power of recollection. For me, it was the laughing that never went away.

"Indelible in the hippocampus is the laughter." This comment, which I made when trying to navigate the peculiar experience of being interviewed by a room full of senators about a high school incident, has now become a slogan printed on coffee mugs and tote bags.

As a strange side effect, people now think I'm an expert in neuroscience and sexual assault. People come up to me and ask, "What happens to the brain when someone is sexually assaulted?" It's complicated; I can't really say, "I don't know," because I sort of do. I suppose if I weren't in the science field, I'd be more comfortable explaining my understanding of it, but as a scientist, you don't talk about something if it's not your true focus.

But that doesn't work outside the ivory tower. I can't look people in the eye and tell them to go read this study from the *American Journal of Psychiatry*. In any case, do they *really* want to know what happens in the brain during a sexual assault? Perhaps there's a sort of comfort in classifying something so chaotic and disruptive within the confines of brain circuitry. Or perhaps what they're really trying to say is, "That happened to me too."

The few times I've given a lecture or spoken at private events, there's a line of people afterward who want to say something to me. They mostly want to tell me that they've been assaulted. They want to tell me the story of their rape or molestation or harassment. My adviser tells me I don't need to talk to them. But I can't just walk away when I know what they want to tell me and why they need to say it.

When those people ask me about sexual assault and how to process it, I don't get into my level of expertise, nor do I answer the question directly. I usually respond with, "I'm so sorry that happened to you." I try to get back to a personal conversation. I can see their pain, but I can't always relate to it. Everybody experiences trauma differently, and unfortunately what happened to me in high school has been eclipsed by what I've gone through the last few years. Being retraumatized has made the original wound much worse. I was not as messed up by it in earlier years as I am now. It probably wouldn't even have come up if I hadn't ended up in couples therapy over a home remodel.

AM I THE only one who has almost gotten divorced over a home renovation project? From about 2007 through 2012, Russell and I had slowly been remodeling the house we'd bought in Palo Alto—which we had barely been able to afford but which probably should have been a teardown. Our lives had become an unending series of decisions about paint colors, materials, and costs. Both of us were over it, but the project itself was far from over. Russell would call me from the hardware store, holding a thousand different paint samples in his hand, and I'd tell him, "Ask whoever works there what they think, and go for it." Even I had met my quota on overcomplication. It was the low point in our marriage, and I love Russell enough to admit it, because we've had far more high points overall.

So we found ourselves sitting in a therapist's office, working on our communication issues. The therapist was a man who looked to be in his early sixties, with graying hair and a hunched-over posture. Books lined his entire office, and, judging from the titles, I noted that he probably did a lot of work with people in substance abuse recovery. His approach to therapy emphasized the importance of people telling their stories. He told me and Russell that in that day's session we would each share a story of something that had happened to us in our past. The only rule was that we could not interrupt the other person until they were done with their story, not even to comfort them. Russell went first and talked about the origin of some issues he had that stemmed from his childhood. I listened to him, and my heart ached for Russell as a boy.

Then it was my turn. I took a breath and told the story of being attacked in high school. I cried a little, but I didn't falter. I relayed it matter-of-factly, all the while still thinking about Russell's story and feeling bad that he'd gone through something that, in my mind, was much worse than what I had. When I finished, I looked up at the therapist. His eyes looked like they were about to pop out of his head. This is someone who is professionally trained to not show any emotional reaction to a client's story. I glanced over at Russell, who had tears in his eyes as he put his hand on my leg.

At the end of the session, the therapist referred me to individual therapy. I figured it was customary follow-up protocol, to tie up any loose ends and move on. I noted that he didn't refer Russell to individual therapy, but I was also open to whatever he thought would be helpful. "Sure," I thought. "Can't hurt." I didn't think of myself as a trauma patient, any more than any other woman who has had to deal with getting groped on the subway or being flashed on the street. It wasn't until I met with the individual therapist and she asked me about my sexual assault that it occurred to me that I'd been thinking of it all these years as an "attack," never seeing it for what it really was, an actual sexual assault. But with this new lens through which to look at it, suddenly the years I'd spent struggling after that night made a lot more sense.

The Bad Years

After the summer of 1982, things went downhill for me. I had no idea what I wanted to do with my life, which is a normal problem for teenagers but becomes worrisome in a place where a fully mapped-out life path is constructed before you even move out of your parents' house. Aimlessness was not an option.

If you'd asked me what I wanted to be when I grew up, I would've probably said the girlfriend of a rock star. (Not a rock star myself, of course.) Most people my age were really into Michael Jackson and eighties music like Culture Club, Duran Duran, and Hall & Oates. I, on the other hand, listened to DC101, the classic rock station, and loved music from the previous decade—Ozzy Osbourne, the Who, Led Zeppelin, and Pink Floyd.

When pressed, I usually said I wanted to become a lawyer someday. I had studied two senatorial campaigns in the 1984 election year for a school project and enjoyed my US government and political science classes. But when I got accepted to the University of North Carolina at Chapel Hill (high SAT scores, not remarkable grades), I essentially said screw it. I didn't care anymore. I checked out. I stopped doing homework and decided to take my senior slump to its furthest limit.

Nevertheless, I made it to Holton-Arms School graduation, where all the girls stood onstage in what looked like white wedding dresses. Each student's name was called, followed by a list of achievements and the announcement of what university they would be attending in the fall. I was delighted to have been accepted from out of state to North Carolina, and the promises of freedom and anonymity were thrilling.

That fall, my dad drove me to college in his big boat of a Cadillac and took a picture of me to mark the occasion. I look miserable in the photo, clearly embarrassed to be seen taking a picture like it was the first day of kindergarten and increasingly overwhelmed by going from a class of sixty kids to a campus of over twenty-two thousand. My dad kept making a show of his departure, clearly stalling and hesitant to leave me.

"You're sure you're okay, Chrissy?"

"Yes, Dad," I assured him. "I'm fine. Go, go."

I urged him off, not wanting to be seen as a baby to my peers as I had been in DC. But I *was* a baby, still only seventeen. As I watched him drive away, I felt a sense of dread and complete unpreparedness for being on my own.

THE CULTURE SHOCK in going from the small, tight-knit brattiness of an all-girls school to a coed college was an upheaval similar to the one I'd experienced when I switched from public to private school, but in reverse. Suddenly I was mostly surrounded by people who had never set foot in a country club. I remember going to my first college party in a preppy polo shirt, only to be surrounded by guys who weren't even wearing shirts. Someone had passed out in a car outside, and I was terrified that they would end up dead. "Should we call the police?" I wondered, while everyone else drank their beers, completely unbothered.

I hadn't yet developed the social skills to make friends who were unlike me, because the insulated world I'd grown up in had placed me with similar kids from similar backgrounds. So of course, when I faced the initial discomfort of making friends in uncharted territory, I just found other people who had come from my town. You can take the girl out of the country club, but you can't take the country club out of the girl, right? I linked up with Adam, a guy I knew who had gone to Landon, and clung to him like a koala to a tree. I think I spent the first two weeks of school sleeping over in his dorm room because I was so petrified of the new environment. People thought we were a couple, but besides a few hookups throughout college, we were just really good friends. He was my security blanket.

College was also a headfirst plunge into the South. I had no lay of the land, and southern traditions made me feel like a foreign exchange student. Guys would show up at sorority houses with a ring or necklace to formally ask a girl on a date. The girls were disarmingly nice, oozing with a sincere sweetness that felt pure and instinctual. No one had ever described me as sweet, much less pure. I'd find out much later that the southern girls did all the "bad" things I did but were just better at hiding it. At the time, though, I looked at myself alongside them and concluded that I was a bad person, which then became a sort of self-fulfilling prophecy.

Though Chapel Hill as a town was traditional and old fashioned, the school itself was quite liberal, and suddenly I had a lot more exposure to Democrats. Lots of protests were happening, including one where the students reconstructed the Berlin Wall in the middle of the quad and students had to scramble around it to get to class. Jimmy Carter spoke at our college and was hailed as a hero.

I befriended a beautiful, very feminist Democrat named Catherine. She taught me a lot, especially that I deserved much better than the guys I was dating. I started to feel a little less lost. Catherine gave me confidence and brought me out of my shell. Then I was assigned to a triple dorm room with two other very dysfunctional girls, in a tiny space the size of an Amtrak car, with a bathroom down the hall. In order to escape, I started to go out every night.

I'd tried mushrooms and pot occasionally before, but now also explored MDMA, which helped me get outside of myself. I had no idea that years down the line I would be designing studies and doing consulting work on the antidepressant qualities of psilocybin and MDMA. At the time, I just knew that they seemed to call bullshit on everything, including my self-esteem issues. They quieted the voices in my head that told me I was unattractive and unworthy, countering with, "You're not terrible, actually." I realized that I had quite a few positive attributes, not the least of which was my ability to have fun. So I leaned into it.

I never got into anything harder, since cocaine didn't help with my anxiety and heroin never crossed my path until I was out of college, and by that point I'd kind of missed the window of experimentation that heroin would have required. So doing drugs recreationally never devolved into addiction. But late-night parties meant I slept through a lot of my classes. The alarm clock would go off, and I'd hit snooze on repeat.

It kills me now, how much learning I missed out on. Later, in grad school, I resolved to never miss one minute of class, to absorb everything I possibly could. To read all the material even if we weren't going to be tested on it. But for the first two years of college, it was a dangerous mix of being let out of a cage and not knowing where to go upon release.

Puzzlingly, as I increasingly struggled to keep my head above water, I found out that all the friends I was partying with were still doing very well in school. "What the hell, guys!" I thought. "We had an agreement here. Aren't we in this together?" It turned out that even though they were staying up just as late as I was, they weren't snoozing their alarms. They were double majoring and getting good grades.

Meanwhile, I was failing all of my tests. I went from straight A's to academic probation in two months. My parents were alarmed. I told them that I would buckle down, that I actually really enjoyed a few of my classes, like geology and mythology.

"Geology?" my dad kidded. "That's the dumbest class I've ever heard of. What're you going to do, work for an oil company? And mythologies? Sitting around and talking about made-up people?" He presented me with options: business, premed, or prelaw. I chose business, which meant taking statistics. It sounded about as interesting as studying car insurance contracts. I didn't take any of my business classes seriously. One day a friend came up to me and said, "The stats teacher called you out today."

"What?" I was caught off guard, even though it was no surprise to me that I had missed class (again).

"Yeah," he went on. "She told everyone in the whole auditorium, 'I'm available if anyone wants help. And there's one person who has literally never come to class in the last month. If you're out there, please come see me.'"

I was beyond embarrassed. And unfortunately, it had the opposite of its intended effect. I felt so much shame that there was now zero chance I would meet with the teacher or even show up in that class again. I figured I had no choice but to take the F.

My parents eventually took my car away, which didn't exactly help because I lived on the far end of campus and now it was even harder to get to class. Then they threatened me with the ultimate punishment, having to go home and transfer to University of Maryland.

I didn't want to go home. I didn't even want to stay in North Carolina. But I realized that getting into grad school would be my ticket out, the only way I wouldn't get stuck. At the end of my junior year, my friend Grant made a suggestion that would alter the course of my life.

"Psychology," he said. "You can major in psychology. That's the only way you'll get out in four years."

I CHOSE IT as my major and turned everything around my senior year. I cut out all vices except for a little drinking and pot. I started going to every class. I loved biological psychology, also referred to as neuropsychology, which is basically the study of how synapses in the brain send messages to your body. The idea that there was this centralized engine driving all of us in such complex ways, and on such a microscopic level, was fascinating to me.

Then I took what we called abnormal psychology at the time, now called psychopathology, and became a little obsessed with it. My teacher was a grad student who couldn't have been older than twenty-four, but he seemed so cool and worldly, a kind of handsome, hippie-looking dude with a beard and mustache who made learning about mental disorders feel like an adventure. We'd go through the encyclopedia of all the disorders and learn how delusional disorder, schizoaffective disorder, and schizophrenia were different; how to parse out the distinctions between major depression with psychotic features; how they all look alike but are not the same thing. We'd learn the nuances of the mood disorders, the anxiety disorders, the biologically based disorders. I thought it was the coolest thing you could possibly study.

I was still getting used to being a good student, though, and I completely missed the memo on a paper he'd assigned. I felt the embarrassment I remembered from statistics class as he walked around collecting everyone's papers. But this time I went home and wrote the paper anyway. I studied really hard for the next test, and as he passed them back, mine landed on my desk with an A at the top. It was the first time I was truly stoked about a grade.

"I want to do this," I told myself. "I want to be a clinical psychologist." Of course, I didn't know at the time that this was probably the hardest graduate program to get into, and I hadn't achieved this clarity about what I wanted to do until I was a senior. Thankfully, Greg had been right about psychology being my only hope, because unlike most of the other majors, which had a linear curriculum that required taking one class before you could take the next, psychology allowed students to take everything at once. However, to get into grad school, you still needed a 4.0 GPA or a near-perfect GRE. The GPA was clearly not going to happen, but I doubled my class load and got straight A's anyway.

You also had to have research lab experience, so I walked into the National Institutes of Health (NIH) campus in the Research Triangle and volunteered for any lab that would take me—the most brazen act I'd taken as a student thus far. They gave me a desk and a group of rats, and I spent two days a week conducting brain and memory experiments, timing the rats as they ran through mazes.

I had never had a clear idea of what I was doing with my life, but suddenly it was like I was a programmed robot. No matter what, I would get a PhD in psychology. I cracked the GRE, earning a perfect score on one of the sections.

My parents bought me a nice typewriter, and I finally felt like a real student. Maybe I'd succeed after all. My dad was still skeptical of psychology, pointing out that he didn't know anyone at the NIH and so wouldn't be able to get my foot in the door at any postgrad programs. To me, that was the point. Academia was refreshingly anti-nepotism. It would not have mattered if my dad had been the head of the psychology department at Harvard—that wouldn't turn me into a scientist. It suddenly dawned on me why I had been given a menu of just three career options: those were careers with a solid job market and high-paying salaries, and they were also the industries that he could help me get into.

"Psychology's different, Dad," I said. "Even if you did know somebody, that kind of thing doesn't work in that field."

"Ah, so of course you chose something like that," he replied.

It felt like I was being simultaneously teased and also finally acknowledged for who I really was, the self-made adult I was becoming. My own person.

I KNOW THAT in the grand scheme of things maybe my "bad years" weren't so bad. But I had a lot of shame around them, the specter of a ghost following me around and telling me that I somehow had less value. It's clear looking back on the arc of my life that something had thrown a wrench into things early on and sent me on a bit of a tailspin. It's not as if what had happened that night in high school was constantly in the back of my mind—far from it. But something significant had changed in me when that happened, a subtle thought that had taken seed, blossomed, and colored my entire self-perception.

I had told myself that only someone who was, for lack of a better word, pathetic would be the target of that type of attention. They wouldn't have done that to a girl who was prettier, more popular, stronger.

It's a ridiculous line of thinking, but I had a teenage brain. Now I know that sexual assaults can be, and often are, random. But back then I thought it had happened because I was a little bit of a loser. I showed up to a party because I was so excited to be invited. But those boys didn't take me seriously, and thus, no one else would.

Psychology finally gave me a reason to be taken seriously *and* take myself seriously. I got into two different grad schools:

the University of Maryland and Pepperdine in Malibu, California. One was thirty minutes away from my hometown; the other was on the opposite side of the country. I looked at the Pepperdine pamphlet, which showed a large cross sitting on a mountainside against a big blue ocean. It all made sense. I would go for a master's in California. And I would be perfect.

The Perfect Years

I had spent a lot of my childhood trying to be the favorite child. It only took me two decades and a move across the country to finally achieve it. For the next few years, my parents proudly gushed over how well I was doing and what a cool Los Angeles lifestyle I was living. Even if I'd gone through some rough patches to get there, I felt like all I needed to do now was maintain the approval I'd sought for so long.

Perfection wasn't just an ideal I was aiming for, though; I pretty much needed to ace every class going forward to balance out my transcripts from undergrad and get into a clinical psychology PhD program, which some people said was harder to get into than med school. They only accepted something like seven people per university. These days, if any of my current students came to me with the academic record I had back then, I would politely tell them to try something else. But at the time, I figured I could lean into my perfect years as hard as I'd leaned into my bad ones. I studied relentlessly. I read everything listed on every syllabus. I would not accept anything less than 100 percent.

Clinical psychology has two routes: you can be a therapist or a researcher. I was still most interested in abnormal psychology, and my practicum work—shadowing professional psychologists in real settings—allowed me to see in action what I'd only read about in books. We worked in Compton with severely mentally ill patients whose issues were exacerbated by socioeconomic inequality and systemic racism, and then we went to Cedar Sinai to work with a totally different, much more privileged population who were suffering nonetheless. It was an obvious discovery, but I was piecing together that when you actually work in the field, it's quite different from just studying psychology from afar. You could go the therapist route and get a master's in social work or counseling, only to spend most of your time trying to figure out how to help someone get bus money and get to their job consistently. It requires a lot of face-to-face interaction helping people with severe trauma. Forming those kinds of relationships with clients can be scary for a beginner.

I loved the philosophy of science—the ability to ask questions about what all of it means and how it evolved. "Can I just keep learning about psychology?" I wondered. Turns out, that's not a profession. Thankfully, there was the research path. I was happy to stay behind the scenes. All I needed to do was maintain perfection for a few more years.

Luckily, it was easier to be perfect in California. For the first time, I'd been plopped into a new environment and felt *more* comfortable. Not to say the move to the West Coast hadn't been a huge leap. A lot of people from my hometown called California "the land of fruits and nuts," and not in reference to its produce.

But it suited me. Pepperdine was located in Malibu, a gorgeous beach town situated on a twenty-two-mile strip along the Pacific. Malibu was a sort of anti-Hollywood, anti-Beltway utopia, not built upon an incestuous network of "who knows whom." It was freeing. It fit.

I had a tiny studio right by the beach and found myself going down to the water daily. I started to recognize the surfers and was intrigued. There was also no real nightlife in Malibu, so the only place to get a beer at the end of the day was the iconic dive Neptune's Net. After hours of studying, I'd grab a drink there and see many of those surfers. We were regulars at all the same places: the beach and the bar. Before long, I started hanging out with all of them and dating one of them.

My boyfriend, Cody, had long hair and a kind soul. Our dates consisted of him teaching me how to surf and us bumming around with the other surfers, mostly guys who lived in rented rooms way up in the hills. They'd come down in the morning, spend the whole day at the beach, grab a drink or smoke a joint at sunset, and trek back up the mountain. Some had suspended licenses or a stack of unpaid parking violations that they just didn't deal with because it would have required going to the DMV in Santa Monica, while the only driving they did was to Oxnard or Rincon to surf. I saw where I could be useful and became the one who drove all the guys around. Who knows what they really thought of me, a girl in grad school tagging along with them, but they couldn't argue with a free ride. They were all loosely employed, working jobs in construction or bartending or, if they really had their shit together, set construction in Hollywood or Caltrans positions standing on the highway with a "Slow Down" sign from 2:00 a.m. to 6:00 a.m. and making twenty-five dollars per hour. But no matter their situation, work never seemed to get in the way of surfing. They were my derelict friends. My "Derryls."

Even though it was about as far away as you could get from the country club scene, these guys had a familiar hierarchy that I recognized from growing up in DC. At the top of the pyramid, there was the best surfer whom no one messed with. But unlike the most powerful men in the East Coast circles I'd grown up in, the person at the top of the surfing hierarchy could also be someone who was missing the majority of their teeth. There was no correlation between profession or background and someone's status. In fact, the best surfers were often the ones who didn't have a job or a penny to their name, because that meant they could be out surfing every day.

I found my spot in the pecking order, first by being Cody's girlfriend, then by having a car and the willingness to drive everyone up and down the coast, and finally by paddling out on days when the conditions were way beyond my skill level and taking waves that I had no chance of making.

I'd started out on a used, bright yellow longboard I bought for about seventy-five dollars. It had dings all over it—boards back then weren't made from the tough epoxy they use now. After about a month, Cody told me I needed to have a board made for me. It sounded expensive, and I objected, but he assured me that he had a guy in San Diego named Peter Benjamin (a.k.a. Beenjammin') who could shape one for me that would be cheaper than the boards on the rack. Soon enough, I had a custom-made fuchsia longboard with white rails (the edges you hang on to), which I promptly snapped in half on my first surfing trip to Hawaii.

It was during a big set at Rocky Point, where all the really good surfers went because it's probably the most consistent left point break wave on the North Shore. I had taken up my position a little bit off to the side in a more beginner-friendly spot, but the waves were still huge. I got thrashed inside one, and when I came up for air, I saw one piece of my board floating off to my left and the other floating off to my right. I grabbed the piece on my left, its scratchy edges where it had snapped shredding my palms. One of the guys, a young phenom I'd been told about, paddled over and asked if I needed help.

"No thanks," I responded automatically, rejecting any sort of assistance out of pride and an instinctual embarrassment.

"Actually, yes," I said a few seconds later. He effortlessly retrieved the other half of my board and helped me get to shore.

Cody came in when he saw what had happened, and he bounded out of the water shouting, "Fuck yeah! That's awesome!"

I was devastated that I'd ruined my board and furious with myself. But Cody was . . . stoked?

"It's not awesome," I said, trying not to cry.

"It's a rite of passage!" Cody assured me. "Some people have a ceremony when it happens and burn the board on the beach at night."

"What? No!" I responded. "I'm going to have someone put it back together."

"Don't bother," Cody said. "It'll never ride the same again."

Cody kept telling me to move on, to consider it a sacrifice to the surf gods. But I paid to bring the shattered board back to

California. I couldn't bear to part with it, especially after it had sacrificed itself on my behalf.

Aside from the broken board, the Malibu years were perfect, but more to the point, they were perfectly imperfect, and that's what finally felt right. All the things that had mattered on the East Coast—achievements, résumés, social status—were irrelevant here. I downplayed the fact that I was getting my master's and working toward a PhD, not because people would have judged me but because no one really cared. Maybe when we were on a long drive it would come up, but my friends were far more interested in talking about how the latest surf session had gone or if I'd seen the full moon last night. It was deliriously refreshing.

Also refreshing was the mosaic of family structures and dynamics they exposed me to. It was the first time in twenty years I'd ever heard "I don't really like my mom" said casually and without any sort of distress. Almost all of the Derryls had only one parent present in their lives. Some had family members they had cut all contact with or siblings who had punched them in the face at the last family get-together but whom they still met up with regularly. At first, I was astounded and, if I'm being honest, a bit judgmental. But then I realized that for all the dysfunction, they had it better. Where I was from, we had all the decorum but none of the closeness. My new friends all marveled at the fact that my parents were still together, but I envied that they felt free in their family unit. There was a strength in that. My parents came out to visit me and were genuinely happy for me. They'd look around at my idyllic setting and remark, "Who would have thought?" My dad would smile and say, "In my next life, I want to be you."

But I didn't dare let them see my real life there. If we went out to dinner and they told me to invite a friend, I'd ask a class-mate from the graduate program instead of one of the Derryls. I couldn't bear to introduce my old family to my new one. I finally, nervously, introduced them to Cody, who my mom thought was sweet and my dad thought desperately needed a haircut.

MY DAD HAD thought that if he put his family in an environment where everyone succeeds, we would all inevitably succeed. That was the intention, and to be fair, that's what happened. He ended up with three kids who all have graduate degrees and rewarding careers. But I also find it ironic that the people and places he wanted us to stay away from were what I ended up finding in LA. Part of me mourned the fact that if I had just found these people sooner, my life would have been happier and psycholog-ically much healthier. But then again, who knows what that life would have looked like. I still credit my dad with getting me across the finish line with multiple graduate degrees and a life I love. Through it all, he stuck by me—and footed the bill.

My dad would say he supported me more than my brothers because women make less in the workforce. He had worked so hard to have three upstanding kids, and I was most in need of funding to make sure that happened.

After thriving at Pepperdine, with its nurturing small classes and caring professors, I ended up getting into a PhD program at the University of Southern California, USC. I was on the right track toward a career I was good at and passionate about. I had gone from being called "a really smart fuckup" to being talked about as a success story back home. I'd hear about miniature re-unions of Holton-Arms, Landon, and Georgetown Prep, and I'd wonder if the people in my circle were friends with my attacker. Each time they got together, I found an excuse not to go. But for the most part, I didn't dwell on anything negative from my East Coast past. I focused on the present moment.

My visits to Hawaii had convinced me that I needed to live there, so I applied to and was selected for a yearlong internship at the University of Hawaii. I would work as a psychologist in training during the day and then surf against the backdrop of a gorgeous sunset at Tonggs Beach each evening. I never wanted to leave, but there was no getting around it: I had to finish my degree at USC.

When I got back to California, I moved to Point Dume, a nicer neighborhood where I could spy Barbra Streisand's property from my apartment. I also started seeing a guy named Brian who hung out in the local surf scene and came from a well-known Malibu family. I was straddling the previous era with Cody and the Derryls and this new relationship and com-munity that felt more in line with what I "should" be doing. I felt a tug-of-war between my heart, which was with Cody, and my head, which reasoned that Brian would fit in better with my family. I thought it was important to make the "right" de-cision, the one that would keep me on my path of perfection. So I chose Brian. "Growing up means going with the sensible choice," I told myself.

But when I was really honest with myself, I realized that I enjoyed hanging out with Brian's friends more than I did Brian. Some of his buddies soon became my best friends, including

Ken, who worked as a stunt double for the TV shows *Melrose Place* and *Beverly Hills, 90210*. He stood in for Jason Priestley and Luke Perry and had a classically handsome face, which helped, because he never had a dime to his name. There was also Aaron, a construction worker and perhaps the kindest person I've ever known. He lived in a trailer and smoked a ton of pot and had these dazzling, earnest eyes. We had breakfast together almost every morning at the Sandcastle restaurant. Aaron didn't surf but would sometimes go out with us and fish, catching sand dabs and perch as everyone else caught waves.

Ken and Aaron felt like family. Because it was so hard to fly home for the holidays (because of logistics and finances and, perhaps most importantly, because I'd developed a crippling fear of it), I started spending some Thanksgivings and Christmases with them. We'd drink Coors Light, build a fire, play some Jenga. I'd look around and think to myself, "I'm so lucky."

One day in a rare moment when I wasn't surfing or studying, I watched Anita Hill testify on TV during the Supreme Court nomination hearings for Clarence Thomas. I listened in horror as she described the degrading things Thomas had done while working as her supervisor at the Department of Education and the Equal Employment Opportunity Commission. I admired her composure.

I had no idea that I would one day follow in her footsteps. Instead, I simply viewed it through the lens of psychology and my knowledge of the effects of trauma. There was something else, though. Part of me felt a recognition, when hearing her describe in graphic vividness Thomas's sexual advances, his unwelcome descriptions of pornography, his humiliating accusation that Hill had put her pubic hair on his can of Coke. I believed her unequivocally, and I knew personally what it felt like to be made to feel so small and powerless.

At Home in the Water

Malibu was where my life as a surfer began, a life that became the guiding force behind every move thereafter. When I was accepted with scholarships to PhD programs at Iowa State and the University of Miami, I turned them down because neither place had good surf. I chose USC to stay close to the good waves.

During my internship in Hawaii, I found myself even more at home. It was as if the farther west I moved, the safer and more at peace I felt. When the internship ended and I had to board a flight home, I held back tears as we took off. I was used to being terrified on flights, but not sad. It felt as if I were being physically ripped away from the island.

I had fantasies of moving even farther west, inspired by my favorite book, *Mutiny on the Bounty*. Based on a true story, it tells the tale of an abusive captain and his insubordinate crew members, who embark from London on an expedition to Tahiti in 1787. Along the way, tensions rise as the conditions on the ship deteriorate. They finally make it to their tropical island destination, which is obviously amazing compared to how they've been living aboard the ship. Many of the men enjoy the way of life there so much they refuse to set sail again to complete their mission. What ensues is a multipart mutiny against the captain, with a central conflict: Do you stay even though it's a crime to abandon your captain and ship? Or do you follow orders and head back to dreary London?

I loved this story so much I later made Russell and our older son go to the South Pacific for my fiftieth birthday to see the paradise described in the book. As we sat on the beach looking out at crystal-clear waters where we didn't even need a snorkel to see the tropical fish flitting by, our son asked me what I would have done if I had been a crew member on the ship.

"Well, look where we are," I replied, surprised he'd even ask such an obvious question. "I'd definitely choose Tahiti over London."

He considered for a moment before responding, "But you should go back, right? Because it's the law. You could just go back and tell people the bad things the captain did."

At the time, I thought it was sort of cute that he was so idealistic. How could any child of mine not choose Tahiti? It was bewildering, but I cut him slack, figuring it was his eighth-grade innocence that prevented him from choosing mutiny. But I also thought, "Who would put themselves through that? Who wouldn't just hide out in Tahiti for the rest of their lives?" I couldn't imagine feeling that much of a duty to my country that I would sacrifice a life in paradise.

LONG BEFORE I was a surfer, I had been a swimmer and a diver. From the age of six, I was on the local swim team, eventually picking up diving. I dropped swimming and stuck with diving when my mom got tired of driving me to endless swim clubs and country clubs to keep up with both sports.

I never loved playing golf like my brothers. Too many rules. It seemed so slow and boring compared to the rush of jumping off the board, momentarily flying, and splashing into a completely different world, where the water muffled all the sounds around me, until I broke the surface and reentered the atmosphere of air.

It started to get less fun as the years went on and it became more about following instructions from my coach. But suddenly, I questioned it. Why did I have to do everything they said? By the time I was fourteen or so, my boyfriend pointed out the obvious when I told him about diving.

"You're going to stand on the edge of the board, facing *backward,* and jump off *toward* the board?"

In one moment, it stopped being good adrenaline. "I guess it is kind of weird," I realized. It psyched me out. I started to lose more often. I quit pretty soon after because winning is far more enjoyable, but I still did it for fun at the pool. I often wore a bathing suit under my clothes during the summer. I had a bathing suit on under my clothes at *that* party, thank God. Perhaps it's kind of like my armor. Now that I think about it, I still wear a bathing suit almost every day during the summer.

These days, I throw a dress over my suit and slather on sunscreen. I pack my big tote bag with everything I need for the day—my beach tent, chips, nuts, fruit. I load the cooler with PB&Js and Gatorade. I throw everything in the car, which usually means first cleaning out the beach stuff from the day before. I gather the wet suits and turn them inside out for easy entry.

My wet suit is thinner than everyone else's, which is a surfer thing—you try to wear layers as light as possible. In the summer I even try to acclimate and not wear a wet suit at all, which as I get older becomes less and less reasonable.

It's about a fifteen-minute drive from our little shack to the junior lifeguard beach. I set up the tent as quickly as I can so I can get right in the water. It's the best way to start the day. I paddle out, ready for the water to muffle the noise in my head. All I need is one wave. Maybe two.

PART
TWO

The Science of the Mind

You don't set out as an undergrad thinking, "I'm going to be a psychologist statistician." Psychology is the broader way in, and then through a series of twists and turns, you find yourself a statistician who works within a psychological application. What we know as psychology today—the study of the mind and behavior—is a relatively young field, around 150 years old or so. But using math to understand data? That started somewhere between 200 and 1,000 years ago, with advanced agriculture and the need to predict the best times for planting and harvesting crops. From humble beginnings, it's stayed a fairly straightforward, mathematical branch of science rooted in facts and numbers.

There's a popular line of thinking that every person who goes into psychology does it either consciously or subconsciously to help themselves with their own mental issues. I'm not a licensed psychologist—I never took the licensing exam—so I can't psychoanalyze my reasons for ending up in this focus of study. But as a statistician, I can study the data that's in front of me.

Probability is one aspect. We can examine the dice rolls of life and all the permutations that did or did not occur. We can look at risk factors. I know I possess certain markers that often lead to a life centered on studying thoughts, feelings, and behavior. I grew up in an intellectual environment; I've felt like the odd one out in most settings; I'm an anxious person. But the probability that I would become a statistics teacher was very low. I failed my stats class in college, something I don't tell my students until the final class. I also hate public speaking. But standing up in front of students is somehow different. You're allowed to do it the way you want.

I'm a little quirky; in lectures, I like to use words like *gnarly* and lifeguard hand signals to gauge whether my students are following along or in the weeds. Sometimes I stop in the middle of a particularly dense subject and ask if everyone's with me. If a lifeguard needs assistance out in the water, they raise their arm and wave their hand back and forth. So if one of my students does that, I know I've got to come over and get them unstuck. But if I ask everyone, "Are we good to move to the next slide?" and they all make a closed fist and tap the tops of their heads (lifeguard speak for "all good") or give me the shaka (more commonly known as the "hang loose" gesture), that means we are on the same page, no need for rescuing.

Perhaps I ended up in my field against all odds. Or perhaps it was inevitable. Common lore in psychology asserts that many of us who end up in the field were the most sensitive ones in our families. We might not have had our emotional needs met. We observed the circumstances around us from a spectator's point of view. We developed skills that helped us handle the disconnect between our external and internal selves. Psychology presents an opportunity to learn about ourselves—research becomes "me search." We are drawn to psychology as a way to help others but also to heal ourselves.

The Corroborators

After I finally told the story of my attack in the couples therapy session with Russell, I started to freak out a little. It had all begun to sink in, and yet the more real it became, the more I couldn't believe it had actually happened to me. What was I supposed to do with all this grief and pain that had sprung up too late? How was I supposed to process it and, more importantly, move past it?

Around the same time, I stumbled upon a photo of George W. Bush at the wedding of his longtime aide . . . my attacker. "Wow," I thought. "Here I am working two jobs and going to therapy and he's hobnobbing with the most powerful person in the world." This was when the internet wasn't what it is now, so I wasn't able to look up much else about him, but it was clear that he was on his way up the ladder and that if he continued on the track he was already on, he could likely end up on the Supreme Court. Seeing his ascent in such a public way was dredging up feelings of rage one minute and ambivalence—or more likely avoidance—the next. It was the most upset I'd been about the incident since it had happened decades earlier.

I decided to reach out to my friend Carisa, whom I had

become close to ever since our kids started kindergarten at the same Spanish immersion school. We always ended up next to each other at school activities, and I was struck by the quiet and approachable kindness that radiated from her. Soon her family was coming over to my house for BBQs and pumpkin carving.

"Can you meet me?" I texted Carisa without explanation, using the busy-working-mom shorthand for "This is important." She was about ten miles south in Sunnyvale, so we looked up the halfway point between us: a Starbucks next to a movie theater in Mountain View. We both pulled up around 3:00 p.m. and saw that next to the Starbucks was an Italian restaurant with a bar. We looked at each other and made a wordless change of plans.

Carisa's job requires her to save all of her receipts, and she still has the one from that day. It shows that I ordered a whiskey neat, which is so out of character that I can only assume I was trying to find strength somewhere in my glass. I was clearly rattled, and we skipped past small talk. I told her what had happened in high school, that the guy who did it to me was now some big-shot federal judge, and that between my therapy session and those wedding photos with George W. Bush, it had kind of spun me out and I wasn't sure how to process it.

Carisa was quiet as she listened. Only when I stopped talking did I stop to think, "What am I doing, rambling on to my very busy friend in the middle of the workday?" I started to apologize for wasting her time, but she stopped me.

"Christine, you don't need to apologize," she said. "Something really bad happened to me too, many years ago."

I stared back at her dumbfounded. Here was the woman whom I had stood next to at Halloween parades as our little superheroes and pirates marched by, whom I had attended bounce house birthday parties with, and who had let me borrow an extra pair of pants when my son had an accident at the spring carnival. That she carried something so heavy around with her blew my mind. I couldn't have known when I reached out to her, but I'd found the perfect person to validate my experience. But my heart also ached for her and what she'd had to go through.

I don't remember much else of what was said that day. But what I'll never forget was the understanding. Telling Carisa felt so different from when I'd shared the story with Russell or the therapist. It reminded me of the silent recognition I sometimes received from other moms when my kid was having a meltdown at the grocery store—but much, much darker. Or the solidarity I felt when I got into the water with another surfer, someone I didn't know but whom, in another more important way, I perfectly understood.

IT HAD TAKEN me a while to build up a friend group in Palo Alto. I had Carisa, and I had work friends who would drag me out for the occasional happy hour, but I hadn't found *my people*, like I'd found in Malibu. When I was in Southern California, I'd hidden my intellectual side to avoid creating a divide between me and my bohemian beach bum friends. I buried the side of myself that liked to talk about *The Odyssey*, in exchange for having the time of my life. It was totally worth it.

Now in the Bay Area, I had to switch over to an entirely intellectual environment, and that meant I had to trade in all the fun I'd had down south. It was not a fair trade. I'd complain to Russell that I didn't connect with the people here; I didn't have anything in common with them besides the fact that they were all workaholics and I was becoming one too. But many of the people in Palo Alto seemed a little over the top, all trying to prove themselves to each other. It felt like we lived in a tight-knit, perfect little village that had absolutely no soul.

Until one day, when I came home and told Russell, "I met a cool person!"

"Wow," Russell responded, sounding surprised and skeptical. "Who?"

"That really disheveled-looking dad who's at the school basketball games sometimes," I replied excitedly. I've always gravitated toward the grungy people in fancy environments. As a teenager, when my family hung out at the country club, I'd end up chatting with the golf caddies or the pool maintenance people. At academic conferences, I'd always drifted toward the people in sneakers, the ones doodling during the PowerPoint presentation. The rejection of pretentiousness comforts me.

"I talked to him today," I told Russell. "And you're not going to believe this—he's a *lawyer*! He went to Amherst! He's super nice, though. And he hates all the things I hate."

That was enough to make us kindred spirits, and we became fast friends. Keith had come from wealth but usually wore the same faded black T-shirt with the Constitution printed across it and a huge hole in the armpit. He carried himself in an unassuming way, glasses slightly askew, stubbled chin, curious, gentle, quick to poke fun at whatever people were taking too seriously, whether it was a kids' Little League game or a school fundraising event where nearly every car in the parking lot was a Tesla. He joked that he and I were in the same club—in recovery from growing up around rich people. That's why neither one of us ever had our hair neatly in place or wore fancy shoes.

One day in 2016, when I was at a Little League game with Keith, we were talking as we usually did, sitting side by side and facing the field. Perhaps it was that low-key setup that made me feel comfortable enough to bring up something that was troubling me. A Stanford student and athlete, Brock Turner, had sexually assaulted a young woman, whose name was kept anonymous at the time but who was later revealed to be Chanel Miller, a twenty-three-year-old Palo Alto woman who had attended a Stanford frat party. The attack had happened on campus, behind a dumpster, while Miller was unconscious from alcohol consumption. Thankfully, two graduate students stopped the assault and restrained Turner until police arrived. He pleaded not guilty in the highly publicized trial, during which his athletic career was constantly brought up, as were the consequences the trial and possible jail time would have on his life. I was saddened but not surprised, considering where I'd come from and how I'd seen young boys' reputations protected. But as the media and seemingly everyone in Palo Alto kept talking about the repercussions for Turner, I couldn't stop wondering, "What about the victim?" And why was everyone so preoccupied with the fact that both Turner and her had been drinking, like that made it somehow justifiable? Clearly, it hit a little too close to home, and when the verdict arrived, with conviction on three felony sexual assault charges but only a six-month jail sentence, it left me feeling physically ill.

I told Keith how messed up it all was. We talked about it from a legal standpoint since Keith was a lawyer. I asked him how a trial like that works and how the sentencing could have been so light.

"It's all up to the judge," Keith said, shaking his head.

"Ugh," I replied. "I have a bad association with judges."

Then without having planned to, I told Keith I'd been attacked at a party in high school, by a seventeen-year-old boy with a "promising future," now a man who had gone on to become a powerful judge in DC. I told him that I had recently looked him up, that he was highly successful in the legal world, that he'd been an aide to Bush, and that he had worked on Ken Starr's Clinton impeachment.

It was a very different conversation from the one I'd had with Carisa. I didn't allow myself to get emotional. Keith wasn't rattled by my confession, even though up until this point we'd mostly stuck to comments on free throws and batting averages. He also didn't press for more details. Then one of our kids got a good hit, and we leaped up to cheer, and that was that.

My KIDS PLAYED a lot of basketball in the street in front of our house, which meant I would frequently have to go out to retrieve forgotten balls from the gutter or from across the street. During one of these trips to recover an abandoned basketball, I ran into my friend and longtime neighbor Rebecca, who was walking her two dogs. This was 2017, when the #MeToo movement was prompting women all over the world to post stories of their own harassment and assault. Rebecca had posted on Facebook about something that had happened with a very powerful and influential man she worked with. I flagged her down and said, "I saw your post. I'm so sorry that happened to you. Are you okay?"

"I'm fine, I'm fine," she answered, waving her hand as if swatting a bug away. "I don't know if I should have even posted that. He's kind of a big deal."

"Well," I said, "I'm glad you posted it. Seems like there are a lot of powerful men doing stuff like this."

"There are no consequences, huh?" she said. "These guys just get away with whatever."

"Tell me about it," I said. "Something like that happened to me too. And my guy is a big-time federal judge in Washington, DC, now."

We went back and forth a bit, comparing the impressive résumés of our respective attackers before switching back to small talk about our husbands, our kids, the neighborhood.

These conversations with Carisa, Keith, Rebecca, and the few other people I'd told over the years faded into the periphery of our friendships, never staying front of mind but swirling around in the background. Until 2018. I emailed Keith from Santa Cruz in the lead-up to the Supreme Court nomination and told him the guy from high school—*that* guy—was a potential candidate for the vacant Supreme Court seat. Keith responded right away: "I remember you telling me about him, but I don't remember his name. Do you mind telling me so I can read about him?"

I wrote back: "Brett Kavanaugh."

Multiple Choice

I hate making decisions. I'm quite possibly the most ambivalent person on the planet. My friends know not to ask me where I want to go for lunch.

And now I found myself in a tortuous maze of decisions, navigating unending questions in a political labyrinth I had never wanted to explore. I'm fifty-fifty on just about everything (the best-case scenario is getting me to fifty-one–forty-nine), so I ended up choosing two options: placing a call to the office of local congresswoman Anna Eshoo and, when I didn't hear back immediately, calling in an anonymous tip to the *Washington Post*. (For all the theories about how my name was later leaked, it's possible I outed myself from the start: because I used my cell phone to text the tip, it would have been easy for any competent sleuth to trace it back to me. At the time, I thought WhatsApp was disguising my identity for me. Live and learn.) It was a Friday, the last business day before the selection, so I figured going both routes meant that, one way or another, it would be on the record before the July 9 nomination. Then I could rest easy, knowing I'd done my duty.

I didn't necessarily see either option as an irreversible act that would change the course of my life. Never in a million years did I think my face would publicly accompany the allegations. I believed I would stay behind the scenes while the appropriate parties took care of it.

You can call me naive. But if you work in journalism or in the public sector, you are (theoretically) supposed to serve truth and justice and uphold the ethics of your job for the greater good of all. Why was I supposed to know the ins and outs of how Congress, the legal system, and high-profile sexual assault allegations work, when there are people who navigate those things as their actual jobs? As a professor, I would never send my students out on their own without explaining the language of research papers and the things you need to watch out for when designing a study or interpreting data. Nor would I ever take someone who had never surfed before, drop them off at Mavericks, and then fault them for wiping out.

So I didn't know I needed a guide. And despite all the conspiracy theories about my political motives in coming forward, I honestly didn't have the luxury of seeing things from such a big-picture point of view. I wasn't very hung up on Brett's politics, knowing that in the grand scheme of things it was Trump's choice and that we would end up with variations on the same theme. I certainly wasn't thinking years in advance to what Brett, as the swing vote on the Supreme Court, would be capable of.

Here's how I saw it: I knew something about one of the candidates, and I thought it was a pretty important piece of information for the president to have when selecting among the possible nominees, especially if there were other people just as qualified for the job. I had never been interested in pressing criminal charges, much less being a liberal operative. Honestly, if it hadn't been the Supreme Court—if my attacker had been running for a local office, for example—I probably wouldn't have said anything, which is a sad, scary thing to admit. But this was a job at one of our most revered institutions, which we have historically held in the highest esteem. That's what I had learned at school and on every field trip as a kid and teenager.

There's a theory in psychology, created by Lawrence Kohlberg, that presents a hierarchical model for the development of moral reasoning: going from infancy and toddlerhood, during which we have no moral compass and only seek to avoid punishment, to childhood self-interest, to the desire to please and help others, to progressing on to personal ethics. At the top level is thinking and behaving according to principle. That's where I sat as I evaluated my choices during this time, and I was under the impression (delusion?) that almost everyone else viewed it from the same perspective. Wasn't it inarguable that a Supreme Court justice should be held to the highest standard? A presidency you could win, but to be a Supreme Court justice, you needed to live your perfection. These nine people make decisions that affect every person in the country. I figured the application process should be as thorough as possible, and perhaps I could be a letter of (non)reference.

On July 5, 2018, I left a message with Eshoo's staff, and the next day, while my kids did calisthenics on the beach with their lifeguard instructors, I sent the following message to the *Washington Post* tip line:

Potential Supreme Court nominee with assistance from his friend assaulted me in mid 1980s in Maryland. Have therapy records talking about it. Feel like I shouldn't be quiet but not willing to put family in DC and CA through a lot of stress

I'd been expecting a quick response, but I didn't immediately hear back from either Eshoo or the *Washington Post*. On July 9, Trump announced Brett Kavanaugh as his selection for Supreme Court justice.

The Lounge Chair Crew

A few days after the nomination, my sons and I came back to Palo Alto, trading one body of water for another as we went to the community pool to dive and swim with our friends every day.

I often thought about how different my sons' childhoods were from mine, and in the next moment, I would become painfully aware of the similarities. The irony was not lost on me that despite all my efforts to escape DC culture, I'd gone somewhere just as political, a place that was also achievement- and status-centric, where I belonged to a swim and tennis club in which my kids could order fries at the pool and just put it on the family tab. I'd thought I had grown up on the lower end of the financial spectrum because of my skewed surroundings, and now my kids had friends who owned horses and went to the Seychelles Islands every summer, and they thus considered themselves to be from a relatively humble background even though they were incredibly privileged. All told, I'd found myself in a very different bubble from the one I'd grown up in, but a bubble nonetheless.

An affluent, progressive bubble of well-meaning but aggressively involved people of influence.

My pool squad consisted of Deepa, a career-oriented mom and force of nature who, when asked what she did for a living, would say she was "just a biotech worker" when she was really one of the best health-care economists in Silicon Valley. There was also Elizabeth, a mom of two and a lawyer. A former prom queen, she was thin and blonde and oozed kindness and optimism. And, of course, there was Keith, who had gone from "disheveled dad" at my sons' baseball and basketball games to one of my close friends.

Most days at the pool, I coached the kids on their diving board techniques and learned the exact spot to throw the football for a perfect running-jump catch. All the kids would be lined up at the diving board steps, with me at the edge of the pool, throwing the football a little higher or a little lower depending on the kid's height and velocity. This summer, though, I was mentally in two places at once, turning around to the lounge chairs between throws to tell Deepa or Elizabeth or Keith, "The senator hasn't called me back yet," and then switching right back to tell one of the kids popping up out of the water, "Good catch! Get back in line!"

The lounge chair crew had come to the beach in Santa Cruz the same day I'd contacted the *Washington Post* and Eshoo's office, and an epic text message thread among Deepa, Elizabeth, Keith, and me had sprung up from that day on through the weekend and into the following Monday, when the nomination was announced. Deepa had sprung into action, suggesting I reach out to Ronan Farrow, the investigative reporter who had exposed the Harvey Weinstein allegations in the *New Yorker* the previous year, or perhaps someone at the *New York Times*, while Keith and Elizabeth repeatedly urged me to hire a lawyer. I reached out to two guys I knew who had also grown up in DC private schools and now lived in Silicon Valley, believing they would inherently understand my unique situation. One of them told me that despite so many people knowing Brett's behavior and drinking habits in high school, I could not do this to my kids. The other one said, "I salute you, patriot."

Keith, Elizabeth, Deepa, and I got into a regular routine: Go to the poolside café, order food, and then head back to the lounge chairs to whisper about politicians and the Supreme Court and discuss whether anyone had called me, what exactly they said, and how I replied. Earlier in the summer we ordered salads, but that soon devolved into endless orders of fries, each of us with our own preferred version (Deepa loved curly, Elizabeth and Keith were shoestring fans, and I usually got sweet potato). The kids would saunter over to grab some fries, we'd pause our conversation until they returned to the pool, and then we'd get right back to it. What would have taken an hour to discuss ended up taking four times as long because of all the interruptions. As a result, from July 15 all the way through Labor Day, we sat in those lounge chairs and typically stayed until the club closed (except for Deepa, who had a demanding job and whose presence was therefore more sporadic). If one of the crew wasn't there by 10:00 a.m., we'd start texting them, "When are you getting here?"

I felt as if I had entered a new era in this whole process, as if the stakes had suddenly been raised exponentially. Deepa spoke about it in much grander terms than Kirsten and Jim had, bringing up the larger issues of feminism and patriarchy.

Society at large was in the midst of the #MeToo reckoning, with A-list actresses coming forward about Weinstein's horrific actions, dozens of women accusing TV journalist Charlie Rose of sexual harassment, and young gymnasts exposing the appalling abuse they'd suffered at the hands of the US national team's doctor, Larry Nassar. I was 100 percent in support of these women and their bravery, but I didn't see myself as part of the movement in any active way, besides my own #MeToo post when everyone was posting their own stories. Even when considering coming forward, I saw myself more as a whistleblower than an activist. I didn't even identify as a "survivor" at that point (but after enduring the testimony and its aftermath, I would change my view).

I also felt a few degrees removed from the other #MeToo accusers because I was going up against the US government. There was no HR department to file a report to, no Instagram campaign to attach myself to. I felt very much like a lone reed in a field instead of part of a collective movement.

One day in August, Deepa told me she had talked to some local women who were politically engaged and active in the #MeToo movement.

"I didn't use your name, of course, no names is the rule," she said. "But I mentioned your situation, and they offered to help, said if you want to talk, they'd love to sit down with you and figure out a way to help."

"Who are these people?" I asked.

"A lot of amazing women," she replied. She mentioned several Palo Alto VIPs from the school board, city council, and tech executives. The only name I recognized was Sheryl Sandberg.

"What? Why would I want to talk to them? I already have my Santa Cruz friends and you guys to talk to. I'm fine," I said. But I couldn't hide my fear and dismay.

"Christine," Deepa said, trying to get through to me, "this is bigger than you. We're talking about the future of women's rights. Everything is at stake with this appointment."

"That's not true!" I said. "It's a conservative appointment no matter what. Have you seen the other people on the list?"

I told her I was not up for talking to anyone who didn't already know. The energy between us was getting tense. I worried that these women, who lived in a different stratosphere of Palo Alto, would find out more about me.

A couple of days later, we were on the stairwell down to the pool carrying french fries and a fresh round of Arnold Palmers for our lounge chair crew and kids. Deepa brought it up again.

"They said you should contact Sherrod Brown," she told me.

"I don't know who that is," I replied.

"He's a senator from Ohio," she said. "And his wife lives in Palo Alto."

She made it all sound perfectly rational, but it seemed ridiculous to me. What was I supposed to do, call up a senator from another state and say that women I don't know in California told my friend to tell me to call you about my problem with the potential Supreme Court justice? I already had met my California representative back in July. She would pass my information along to our senator. Isn't that how it is supposed to work? Hadn't we all watched too many *Schoolhouse Rock* cartoons and been on school trips to the Capitol?

I told Deepa that I had no intention of calling Sherrod Brown. I had faith that the women would continue to abide by "no names." They had big-time jobs and surely other things to do. And I knew Deepa would certainly never share my name.

A few days later, a local woman messaged Deepa saying she'd spoken with one of Silicon Valley's top female social media executives. They conveyed that they were happy to get the name of a good journalist to talk to. They didn't think Eshoo or Feinstein were going to get me anywhere.

Deepa went on to put a menu of options on the table: having the VIPs connect us with a journalist, contacting the senator from another state or reaching out to Ronan Farrow directly. Meanwhile, Elizabeth had talked to one of the senior counsel at her work, who had put in another vote for talking to Ronan Farrow, while also urging me to get legal representation.

The text messages between various high-powered Palo Alto women continued. Deepa let me know through the grapevine that the women really wanted to sit down and talk to me but also really didn't want to be involved. Finally, a bizarre message from the friend of another Silicon Valley executive drifted down to us at the pool lounge chairs.

> *She feels very strongly that this will crash and burn as a "political stunt" unless she gets the right attorney. She thinks the best thing to do is to find the right white, male, GOP attorney who will do this pro bono. If your friend comes out with that attorney, people can't write it off as a political stunt. They'll still try. . . . If your friend can wait a few hours (a day max), she is sure she can come up with the*

perfect attorney to take care of her. And then he
might be able to keep her name out of it for a
while. What do you think of that strategy?

I dove into the pool and swam the length underwater without coming up for a breath. I was better off alone.

The Handoff

It was almost two weeks after getting in touch with Anna Eshoo's team on July 5 that I found myself sitting in the congresswoman's office, on the afternoon of July 18. I wondered if it was even worth being there since Brett had been nominated already—hadn't we missed the window?

At least getting it on record would bring me some closure. I had a pen and paper, mapping out the details for Eshoo's aide, Karen Chapman. She was very friendly and assured me that although the congresswoman was in Washington, DC, I could tell her what had happened and then meet with Eshoo two days later.

I sketched out the room for her. I was here; Brett was there; Mark was over there. Here was the bathroom. Here were the stairs. I explained to Karen how terrifying it had been to be trapped, with only one way to escape the room. I told her that when Brett had put his hand over my mouth to muffle my screams, I could barely breathe and I feared that he would accidentally kill me. She followed along with a grave face. At the end of the meeting, she told me that they would be in touch when Eshoo was back in town. Two days later, I was scheduled to meet with the congresswoman. I was nervous and asked my two colleagues what I should wear.

"Really?" they responded. "That's what you're concerned about?"

They were both high up at Stanford and had met with Eshoo many times in the past. They reassured me that she was extremely nice and that I had nothing to worry about, but I felt like I was back in school again, going on a field trip to a congresswoman's office, even though I'd been there not three days before. This time, though, it was the real deal—I felt like I was crossing a threshold, doing something that couldn't be taken back. The meeting was scheduled for the end of the day on Friday, so Eshoo wouldn't have to cut our conversation short by being pulled into another meeting.

Once I arrived, I realized I shouldn't have worried about talking to a high-powered politician. They of all people know how to make any meeting smooth and cordial. Eshoo greeted me warmly and led me down a hall with what looked like approximately one thousand doors. As we entered her office, she pointed out that the room had multiple exits. "Is this because of what I told her aide?" I wondered. If Karen had already told her the details of what I'd shared, down to the feeling of claustrophobia during my attack, I wondered what we would even have to talk about.

But then Eshoo asked me to describe what had happened in high school, and I found myself repeating the entire story I'd told her aide two days ago. At the end of my recounting, I told her that I was now trying to figure out what to do with the information, that I'd asked friends and colleagues for advice, and that it had been a somewhat confusing process but that I was grateful for her taking the time to hear what I had to say.

"How many people have you told?" she asked.

"Not that many," I said, worried that I'd already made a mistake. It felt like *Washington Post* was tattooed across my forehead. "Just a few close friends."

"You know that story about the little girl on the mountain?" she asked, as if *of course* I knew the story she was talking about. "She blows the petals of a flower into the wind, and they all scatter. And then she wants them back, so she goes around trying to gather them all up, but it's impossible."

I nodded, feeling once again like I was back in school, not quite following the lesson.

"We don't want this to get out of your control," she told me. "Whoever you've told, make a list of their names. And don't add to it."

She then explained constituent confidentiality to me, which meant that as her constituent, anything I told her would remain private information unless I authorized otherwise. I was surprised and wondered what she *could* do if that were the case. What a strange thing, to go into a congressperson's office to tell them something that might affect the integrity of the Supreme Court and have them assure you that they won't tell anyone. I was a bit baffled. I hadn't gone to Eshoo just to have a confidante, after all. I of course wanted my name protected, but I also expected something to come of my disclosure. Now it felt like I'd tried to hand off the football, but it had just been passed right back to me.

She told me she would be talking to a friend in the Senate, who I guessed was Dianne Feinstein, the ranking member on the Senate Judiciary Committee and the longest-serving female senator in history. "Ah, of course," I thought. "She'll take care of it." I left Eshoo's office and went into my weekend, which would be filled with soccer camp, and waited for Feinstein to contact me.

That evening, my mentor at Stanford, whom I called "El Jefe" even though he wasn't technically my boss, called me to check in.

"How'd it go?" he asked.

"It was okay," I said. "I mean, she was great, super nice. But she told me I can't talk about it anymore."

I always told him everything. It felt awkward to suddenly shut that off in this instance.

"Well, I guess there are certain things you just have to do alone," he said, "and this is going to be one of them."

"Do *what* alone?" I wondered. It was still so unclear what would be required. But he seemed unfazed.

"You can do it," he said. "And no problem, we won't talk about it anymore."

The problem was, I couldn't control whether the people I'd *already* told would stay quiet. The list of those I'd told was actually quite small, even though I felt like Anna Eshoo had given me a lecture for talking about it to everyone I knew. Still early in my journey, it was what I would come to discover as the survivor's Catch-22: you're told not to tell too many people, but then later you're told your story isn't credible because you didn't tell anyone. You can't win. It's one of the many ways survivors aren't supported in coming forward. I'd learn a lot more in the weeks, months, and years to come.

Law and Order

On July 26, I traveled with the boys to Maryland and Delaware to visit my hundred-year-old grandmother, who was in hospice. She'd always been a unique person in my life. While my dad was undoubtedly the leader of our immediate family, it was my mom's mom who was the glue of our extended family. She was the center of a family tree that was deeply rooted in DC (like I said, most people never leave), including my aunts, uncles, and cousins, who all gathered at her house for every holiday and celebration.

Maw had always been my prime example of using your life to give back to others. She worked full-time in the cafeteria of an elementary school in Landover Hills, Maryland, up until she was in her nineties. She loved the mostly poor and working-class kids she served breakfast and lunch to and gave free extras when no one was looking. She was awarded a DC public service award for her work. My mom would tell us that she and my dad tried to coax Maw to retire or move closer to our house, even offering to buy her a home, but she had no interest. She preferred to maintain her independence and stay in the house and the community she had served for decades. She was simply the kindest, most generous person, and while it was unbearably sad to be losing her, there was no doubt that she had lived her life exactly the way she wanted and never wasted a day of it.

Between consoling my kids and working out my own grief, I went back and forth with Feinstein's aide, Jennifer Duck, who told me I needed to write a letter detailing my allegations, which could then be hand delivered to Feinstein.

"A letter, like through the mail?" I asked.

"No, you can send an email," she clarified. "But it needs to be in a separate document, attached to an email. Someone will print it out and give it to her in person."

"Okay," I thought. "However she needs things to be done, I guess." I'd already told her, Anna Eshoo, and Karen Chapman the story, but whatever they needed from me in order to do what they needed to do, I was happy to accommodate.

After a few hours with my grandma at the hospice center, I was at my parents' house in Rehoboth Beach on July 30 when I received a call from Senator Dianne Feinstein herself. I rushed into the kitchen so my mom and dad wouldn't hear the conversation. (I thought going through my grandmother's final days was quite enough for them to handle without me dropping the news that I was talking to a senator about disgracing a revered federal judge.)

"Hello, Christine!" Feinstein yelled into the phone. I glanced over at my parents, who thankfully had the air conditioner and the TV blasting in the living room. I quickly put my full focus on answering Feinstein's questions, shouting back into the phone in a bizarre screaming match. It reminded me of talking to my parents, especially considering they were close to her in age.

At one point early in our short conversation, Feinstein asked/shouted with disarming directness, *"Were you . . . raped?"*

I yelled back with my mouth as close to the speaker as possible, *"No!"*

TWO DAYS LATER, my grandmother passed away. I wrote to Emma Brown, the *Washington Post* reporter I'd been cautiously talking to over the last three weeks, and told her that I was going through a death in the family and was tentative about coming forward but that if I did end up going to the press, she was the one I would contact.

Feinstein's aide had also asked me if I was planning to get legal counsel. I had waved this off time and time again. After all, why would I need lawyers if I hadn't done anything wrong? I'd told my congressperson and senator already. Wasn't the ball kind of in their court now? As lawyers themselves, my friends Keith and Elizabeth had been persistent about it too and could probably write a book titled *1000 Ways to Tell Your Friend They Need a Lawyer*. I realized I had now spent (wasted?) six weeks telling people that I didn't need lawyers. Finally, I caved and began to search for legal support.

At first no one wanted to represent me, especially pro bono (I had quickly discovered that my scientist money was not enough to cover lawyer rates). They all rejected me in the nicest ways, saying their client list was full or sometimes being slightly more honest and telling me their associates would be too scared to go up against someone that high up in the judicial system.

I was on the phone with one of the top attorneys in the country, who was giving me yet another very nice rejection, when he said in a thick southern accent, "I have no love lost for Brett. But my associates and I aren't the right people to take this on. I do know someone, though, who's not afraid of the devil. His name is Larry. I'll put you in touch."

Larry Robbins had represented other people who had spoken in front of the Judiciary Committee, something that none of the other lawyers I'd talked to could claim. I called him from the parking lot of a Walgreens in Rehoboth so I could continue to avoid my parents' curiosity. It must have been ninety-five degrees out, with East Coast humidity that made it intolerable to sit in a hot car with the windows down. I parked and kept my car running with the AC on, an act that would have been unthinkable in eco-conscious Palo Alto, though no one seemed to care here.

Larry's voice came on the line, projecting a seasoned gravitas and no-nonsense trustworthiness that felt like a salve considering the past six weeks.

"My partners might have some issues," Larry said. "I'll have to talk this over with them. I will help. Let's talk again in a couple days."

I was next introduced to the legal team of Debra Katz and Lisa Banks, whose names had been on a list of DC law firms that worked with whistleblower-type clients.

For the last week, I had been consumed by a triple threat of anxieties: family, funeral plans, and flying. I would need to drive from Delaware to DC for Maw's funeral, then drive to meet Debra and Lisa in Baltimore before taking a short flight to visit Russell's family in New Hampshire, and then finally head back to Palo Alto. For someone who feels like they might die during every flight they take, that is a lot of travel to handle in such a short time. But Deb (as she typically went by) and Lisa booked a hotel room close to the airport in Baltimore and reserved a conference room for our initial meeting.

As I sat across from Deb and Lisa, I could tell they were clearly studying me. I was as professional as I could be, but visibly nervous. They were, in contrast, seemingly not afraid of anything. Unlike me, they were clearly not ambivalent, but decisive, quick thinking, and efficient. They stepped out at one point to confer with each other. I imagined them saying, "Who is this nutty lady, with the underside of her hair dyed blue?" But when they came back, they asked if I would be comfortable working with them.

Once we signed the paperwork, I was surprised by how relieved I felt. As competent and invaluable as my friends had been, basically acting as my 24/7 on-call consultants, it was nice to have some advisers with DC-specific expertise backing me up. Until that point, it had felt like I was staring at a chessboard, plotting out each possible move, but not knowing who I was really up against or why the stakes were so high. Now I had coaches who knew the game better than I ever would. In addition to Deb and Lisa, I was also able to turn to Larry time and time again for sage advice throughout the next few months. I certainly felt I could use all the help I could get.

The day after my meeting with Deb and Lisa, they arranged for me to take a polygraph test. It took place at a conference table long enough to seat twenty people, but with just me and the test administrator. While I'd felt comfortable enough to give a few male lawyers an overview of the assault over the phone, this was the first time I'd talked about the details in person with a man I didn't know. It was daunting, but I was relieved to be doing something concrete that would hopefully get things moving.

By August 10, I was back in Palo Alto continuing the waiting game. I didn't know that Dianne Feinstein was not taking any action on my letter; I thought she was working behind the scenes and just couldn't tell me what was happening, so in the meantime my lawyers worked seemingly around the clock to figure out what "coming forward" could look like and how I might do it with the least amount of damage to me and my family. Their recommendation was that if I was going to say something, I should do it well before the initial confirmation hearings began on September 4. I couldn't just drop the news on a Friday if he was testifying the following Tuesday. Considering I'd wanted the information to be on record before he'd even been nominated, I agreed: the sooner, the better. But that still left the larger question of how.

Deb and Lisa continued vetting my account of what had happened. I was beginning to get more comfortable talking to the lawyers and following their lead, especially because there seemed to be a lot going on behind the scenes that they were sparing me from. I knew that Deb and her team were spending all morning on the phone strategizing before even talking to me. They were not only figuring out the route they'd take with the Senate Judiciary Committee but also deciding the approach they'd take with *me*. And then after I got off the phone with them, they'd reconvene together and continue strategizing. They were obviously very good at their job. Hopefully they'd lead me through this as painlessly as possible.

The Breakup

We had been drafting three different letters to send to the committee, with varying levels of anonymity or lack thereof. One version would be addressed to Dianne Feinstein and the Senate majority leader, Chuck Grassley, but would not include my name. One would include my name but only be addressed to Dianne Feinstein. And the final, riskiest one would include my name and both Feinstein's and Grassley's names, undoing constituent confidentiality. The first two probably wouldn't get much accomplished, but the third option seemed to just throw me to the wolves.

I felt like I had already gone through a lot to deliver the information to the appropriate parties. I had taken the polygraph test. With a healthy dose of mortification, I had gotten in touch with ex-boyfriends I hadn't talked to in decades in the hope that they might be able to corroborate the story. I first pushed back on this idea, assuring my lawyers that I had been too embarrassed about what had happened in high school to tell anyone until many years later, but I wanted to be cooperative. First I called my high school boyfriend Scott, whom I'd started dating right after the incident with Brett. I spoke to him from the driver's seat of my van, chatting for two hours before we ended the call with him sending me healing vibes (he'd moved to LA and adopted a very Zen way of being). I called Drew, a commercial fisherman I'd dated in Rehoboth Beach, where my family went each summer. I'd swim to Drew's boat to dig up shellfish and sell them to restaurants, swimming back to my parents' house at the end of the day as they sipped chardonnay with their friends on the deck. I did not call Cody from my Pepperdine days, who now lived in Bali. I called Andy, a fellow psychologist and my first friend at Stanford, to whom I'd told so many life stories while we drove along the San Mateo coastline looking for surf. As predicted, none of them remembered me saying anything about what had happened. I had considered it a stain on my character, something to be hidden. In my mind, it wasn't worth telling them if there was a chance they wouldn't like me anymore.

But while going down the list of ex-boyfriends, I couldn't bring myself to call Brian, the guy I'd dated after Cody. Our breakup had been so bad, I didn't want to face him again. I couldn't imagine that he'd even take my call, and in the case that he did, I didn't want to tell him what had happened to me. I figured I'd done the work of calling and was getting concerned about limiting the number of people I told. This last one could slide.

I had also gotten access to my medical records and found the therapist's notes from the couples session with Russell during which I'd described the incident and mentioned that the person was now a federal judge who might end up on the Supreme Court. I had read the notes from my individual sessions with the trauma therapist our couples counselor had referred me to, which referenced the high-profile status of my attacker.

Another task I'd agreed to was to fix the privacy settings on my social media accounts. Karen Chapman, Eshoo's aide, had helped me do it, convincing me that it would protect my friends from reporters and investigators fishing around for more information. Once I heard the words "protect your friends," I basically handed over my phone. I also immediately stopped posting. I never thought social media was particularly import-ant to me, but over the next few days I had strange withdrawals and moments of muscle memory, going to my phone only to realize that I could no longer post every single thing my kids did or every restaurant we ate at (in retrospect, perhaps I was more into social media than I'd thought). "Are my friends won-dering where I went?" I asked myself.

The days dragged on, as the confirmation process continued its course. It felt like I had spent every waking hour working on this, and yet I still found myself racing the clock, trying to avoid handing off the information later in the game than I'd ever wanted.

By August 29, we decided I would include the Republican Senate majority leader Chuck Grassley on the letter we were drafting, undoing the constituent confidentiality that had been in place with Eshoo and Feinstein. My name would proba-bly come out. It might be in the news. The lawyers told me I needed to tell my extended family what had happened and give them a heads-up in case my name went public. I knew this needed to start with my dad, the family member I was closest to and who might hear from someone else otherwise. I didn't want him to be caught off guard.

I left my office at the Stanford Psychiatry Department and sat in the parking lot staring at my phone. I thought back to that night in high school. I'd usually get home not a minute earlier than my curfew, but because I'd rushed out of the party, I arrived home much earlier than usual.

I had opened our front door with a huge noisy creak, which I now know my parents probably intentionally never fixed so that they could clock when I made it home each evening. I tiptoed up the stairs and saw that my dad was still awake, his bedroom door propped open. I tried to slip past without him noticing me. I felt like it was written all over my face.

As I held my breath in the small hallway between our bedrooms, he shuffled out in his light-blue linen pajamas. I avoided looking him in the eye and mumbled, "Yeah, I'm home. Going to bed. Night."

When I finally made it into my room, I felt relieved. I'd gotten invited to a party, I'd dodged whatever would have happened in that room had the boys gotten their way, and I'd made it home without getting in trouble. My fifteen-year-old mind only knew how to focus on the normal teenage concerns, unaware that something far more traumatic had happened and would continue to affect me decades later.

Now, nearly forty years since that fateful evening, my dad picked up the phone, and I finally told him what had happened.

"Are we talking about Brett Kavanaugh?" he replied.

"Yeah," I said, choosing not to linger on the fact that there had been no acknowledgment of what I'd gone through or what impact it had had on me.

"Why is this going to come out publicly?" he asked.

"He obviously knows about it," I said. "And probably some other people from the area do too. There's a strong chance it could end up in the news. So just be ready."

"You know your nephew's on the job market right now," he said.

"I know, Dad," I said. I felt this concern given our unusual last name. "It's not good. I'm going to call him."

"No, no. I'll call everyone. I'll tell them," he said. He sounded stressed. "Are you sure about this, Chrissy? You've worked so hard. You've overcome a lot. You have such a nice family, the boys. Now you're at Stanford. Why put all that at risk?"

"Because it happened?" I couldn't undo that simple fact. "But you know how the twenty-four-hour news cycle works. It'll go away as quick as it came. We just have to survive the twenty-four hours."

That reassured him. "Oh, I see what you're saying," he said. "Trump will probably do something else that will get all the attention, and then it'll blow over."

I was glad to have gotten the conversation behind us, but it still made me uneasy. I knew that the golf club was the center of his world. He's a man who cares about decorum, about being a gentleman and acting decently. In the tight-knit DC scene, especially among his generation, drama was considered uncomfortable and was typically swept under the rug as quickly as possible. I desperately hoped this wouldn't cause him too much trouble.

TWO DAYS LATER, my lawyers called me, speaking faster than usual.

"Christine, our final recommendation is that you don't go forward."

"Wait, when did you decide this?" I asked, looking at the three letters we had been drafting the previous day. We had deliberated over every word.

"Unfortunately, making this public is not going to make a difference, Christine. Chuck Grassley is just going to bury it. Allegations come up during every nomination. This happened so long ago, and it's really not safe for you to expose yourself given all the risks."

Besides the fact that there seemed to be an "Allegations" section for every Supreme Court nomination, which was a bit problematic, to say the least, I was also devastated that I'd spent the last two months trying to do this the right way and now everything had turned on a dime.

"How is this possible? What about all the work we've done?" I said. "I don't understand why you're saying all of this now. It's not what you said when you had me contact my ex-boyfriends. It's not what you said when you made me do a polygraph. It's not what you said when you made me tell my dad *two nights ago!*"

"Wasn't it maybe a little therapeutic to tell him, at least?" they asked.

"No. Opening up a massive wound and then letting him know it would play out in the media? Not therapeutic."

As they continued talking, it got stranger.

"Dianne Feinstein actually needs to close this out. She will be sending a letter, and you need to acknowledge that you've received it."

"What? Are you serious?"

Shortly afterward, the letter arrived on formal stationery. I read in disbelief. Feinstein wrote that she understood I did not want to come forward and that her office would keep the information confidential, not taking any further action unless they heard from me. The letter ended with, "Please convey my deep appreciation to your client for her courage in sharing this information with me and assure her that I understand and regret the deep impact this incident had on her life."

I felt like I'd just received the weirdest breakup letter of all time. My lawyers continued to try to smooth things over. They sent me an official letter telling me they were advising me not to come forward. They insinuated that there was concern over whether I could psychologically withstand the process. They were justified, given that I was teary-eyed during most of our meetings, but I took it defensively. "Obviously I can handle it. I have a solid career and friend network. If I can't take the hit with so many resources, who could?"

"I'm sorry, Christine," they said. "We just can't let you stand in front of an oncoming train."

"What happened to all the talk about doing this for future generations?" I asked. "If that's the case, I'll stand in front of the train."

"You are our client," they responded. "We can't represent future generations. We're all looking out for your best interests, Christine."

"You're not looking out for my best interests!" I finally cried. "I'm out in the middle of the fucking ocean!"

The line went silent as they questioned what I'd said and whether I'd truly lost my mind.

"It's a surfing thing," I explained. "You made me paddle out. That's the hardest part. And you never, ever paddle back in once you're out there. You catch the wave. You wipe out if you have to. You don't paddle in. *I* don't do that. If you're asking me to paddle back in, I don't want to speak to you anymore."

Trying to talk me down, Deb offered to take surf lessons.

"You should want to surf anyway!" I threw back at her. "I can't believe you're doing this to me. I've been working *so* hard."

I couldn't see at the time that they'd also been working incredibly hard, pro bono. I didn't want to acknowledge that Dianne Feinstein was just doing her job.

"Why don't you take some time, Christine. We'll talk soon."

I hung up the phone, crying tears of rage and frustration. I had contacted my representative on July 5, almost two months ago, before Brett was on the short list. Now it was Labor Day weekend and his confirmation hearings were starting next week. If I had just put my name on a letter to Chuck Grassley sooner, it would already be out there. I had hesitated on taking the wave, and now it had passed me by.

It got worse as others learned about the breakup. I told the lounge chair crew that after they had listened to me all summer, nothing was going to come of it. I had been crying nearly nonstop since receiving the letter. Deepa abruptly got up and moved six lounge chairs away from me. I lay on my own lounge chair looking comatose as Keith and Elizabeth did their best to console me.

Keith pointed to the powerful Palo Alto big-wigs around us at the pool.

"Look at all of these big talkers who complain about the state of the country," he said. "None of them would ever have been brave enough to do what you did."

"I didn't do anything," I argued.

"That's not true," Keith said. "You did a thousand times more than what most people would ever do."

Finally, Deepa came back and sat next to me on my chair.

"First of all," she began, "I'm not mad at you. I'm just mad at the whole thing. There's so much on the line. We can't just do nothing."

Anna Eshoo's office called not long afterward and offered to contact then-senator Kamala Harris's office to see if she could push it forward. I thought back to when I had suggested that weeks earlier and they had told me I shouldn't call her. I felt like I was on a merry-go-round and was ready to fling myself off.

"If you want to call Senator Harris, go for it," I told them. "I don't really care."

I had an appointment to see a PTSD specialist the day after Labor Day (the first day of Brett's hearings) to put the trauma of what had happened back in its little box and move on. I would start teaching again in a few weeks and figure out how to live with myself if he got appointed. I decided the only option was radical acceptance of an unwanted outcome.

But other forces were at work that decided otherwise.

It's tough to know exactly what or who was responsible for the events that followed, but one way or another, Feinstein did end up sharing the information with her fellow Democrats. My lawyers were in the Capitol the following week when they happened to pass by the committee room, overhearing a heated argument between the Democratic senators that was quite likely about me and the fact that Feinstein had kept my allegations to herself for so long.

While I struggled with a crushing sense of loss and failure, I started getting calls and emails from journalists looking into "a

Palo Alto woman who had sexual assault allegations against the Supreme Court nominee."

It looked like I would be stepping forward—or rather, tossed forward—after all.

Here Goes Everything

It was comforting to learn that the ethics of journalism dictated that no one could publish the name of a survivor without their permission. But they could still try to track me down, text, call, park in front of my house, and follow me to work down El Camino Real in hopes of earning my trust.

The week of the initial hearings, I watched on TV as Brett entered the room with a parade of women and girls. I couldn't help but think this move was a little strategic, an intentional testament to (or defense of?) his advocacy for women, which I had to admit had been a big part of his professional reputation, as a champion for appointing women to high judicial positions and mentoring many of them throughout their careers. I didn't watch the rest of his initial hearing, but heard from the people who knew my situation that they'd watched and were "not impressed." I didn't say much. After all, my part in all this was over. It was time to see my PTSD therapist, try to move on, get back to work. I'd wasted my summer, missed some good swells, but was feeling relieved that I could work on my syllabus for the fall quarter instead of talking to lawyers for hours on end.

As Brett's hearings came to an end, reporters started showing up at my house, parking outside for hours, occasionally knocking on the door. There was one man in particular, walking up and down in front of the house, who drew the attention of all the neighbors. He had perfect porcelain skin and wore a fancy navy blazer and white pants. The people on my street knew he wasn't someone I would've normally had roaming around outside my home. I took a photo and sent it to Deb. "Oh, that's Ronan Farrow," she said nonchalantly.

"Why don't you just walk out there and tell them, 'Hi, everyone, yes, it's me'?" Russell asked.

"I can't do that," I said. "Besides, they know it's me. That's why they're here."

I was held hostage, periodically peeking out the window only to find that another car had shown up on my typically quiet street. That afternoon I walked into the living room to discover that my younger son had let a reporter from BuzzFeed inside. To be fair, she looked young and harmless. But still, what was he thinking she wanted—to play Fortnite with him? I yelled at her and my kid—something I rarely ever did—telling her to get out and warning my son never to let someone he didn't know in the house. The reporter started sending me text messages asking to talk and articles she'd written that vouched for her work. Her requests to see the letter I'd written to the committee went from friendly to more forceful.

The following Monday was my first day of the new school year, a hectic day for teachers and students. I had just lectured for three hours, and as students were filing out to the hallway, I told them to have a great week and let me know if they had any questions. I heard a woman's voice say, "I have a question." I thought it was a student until I saw her face.

"Do you have the letter?"

It was the same BuzzFeed reporter.

The media still couldn't release my name, but now articles were referring to Kavanaugh's accuser as a "Palo Alto professor," which had people from my hometown sending screenshots to each other and asking, "Is this Chrissy?" It didn't take a detective to put it together.

Some say that after Dianne Feinstein shared the information, Chuck Grassley leaked it to the news site the Intercept. Or perhaps it was someone else on the committee. I've been told Sheryl Sandberg's brother-in-law was the one who called Sherrod Brown. Or perhaps it was one of the other people on the text chain. I'm not sure it really matters. In any case, the information and my name had been leaked.

Since my name would be coming out anyway, my lawyers told me it was time to do a media interview. I was starting to feel like I'd get whiplash from the back and forth between "you need to come forward" and "you absolutely can't come forward," but I agreed to talk to the reporter from the *Washington Post* who had been in touch since my original tip to the anonymous hotline. Emma Brown was a young reporter, certainly not as big a name as some of the other journalists who had gotten in touch with me, but she was the one who had called me back in the first place, and I liked the idea of giving someone less established a chance to break a big story. It seemed like a fitting move to go with an anti-elitism pick (even if she did work for the ultimate elite DC news outlet). She'd also seemed genuinely caring, checking in on my well-being and sending condolences when Maw had passed.

I traveled to Half Moon Bay, where Russell and I had gotten married, to meet with her. I figured a place that held good memories would be a nice antidote to the realities of what we would be talking about. As we started the interview and Emma began recording the conversation, the magnitude began to seep in. We debated how to refer to me: Christine Blasey? Christine Ford? As someone who'd only seen my name in print in academic journals, I found it almost amusing—until my nerves kicked back in.

After our interview, Emma called me on her way to the airport, informing me that the article would be published that Sunday, September 16. Immediately before it ran, they would have to hand the piece over to the White House, and that team would have an hour to review it. She said she needed to ask me a few more questions, ones she really did not want to have to ask.

"Did he take his fingers and insert them in your vagina?" she asked.

"No," I answered.

"Are you sure?"

"Yes, I'm sure."

"Did he try to put any part of his hand in your vagina or anus?

"I'm really sorry," Emma said in the pause before I answered "No."

"What is happening right now?" I thought. "I just wanted to share some information. Now we're at this level?"

I kept Saturday night marked in my brain as the last chance I'd have to kill the story. But Saturday night came, and I didn't back down. By Sunday morning, during the time that the White House was reviewing the article—which ended up taking a *lot* longer than one hour—the opposition research began. I got notifications that my LinkedIn profile had been viewed by someone whose profile boasted that she'd destroyed Hillary Clinton's reputation during the email scandal, as well as a White House lawyer who would go on to popularize a "mistaken identity" theory explaining that I'd confused Brett with someone else.

Clearly, we would need to leave our house and try to lie low. I was already getting death threats sent to my work email. The morning of publication, my friend Chris came to get our dog, and Elizabeth took my younger son to the pool (Russell and my older son were in Lake Tahoe for a soccer tournament). Elizabeth texted me not long after, letting me know that the TVs at the poolside grill, which normally played *SpongeBob SquarePants* on a constant loop, had my face all over them. I got notifications from research sites informing me that a paper I'd coauthored in 1998 had now been downloaded two hundred times (the academic equivalent to suddenly showing up on the bestseller list).

I packed a tote bag with a bathing suit for the pool, some pajamas, and a few extra shirts. I wouldn't be going home again for months.

Hotel California

I booked a hotel room and hunkered down on publication day. Within minutes of the piece going live, text messages from friends started flooding in. Within hours, news outlets began reporting wild claims that I was a deep-pocketed major donor to the Democratic Party (in fact, my donations from the previous five years were less than one hundred dollars in all), that I was a pussy-hat-wearing radical (there were doctored photos and fabricated Twitter posts that made it look like I'd been on some sort of anti-conservative crusade), and that I was currently driving across the country to give my testimony because I was afraid to fly (less far-fetched but still untrue). Then there were text messages and emails from strangers, ranging from "If you testify, we will kill you" to "On behalf of all survivors across the world, we need you to testify."

Within two days, we had to hire security. I had about $20,000 to my name, and while I'd been dead set against using it on lawyers, now I just threw it at securing bodyguards. The former 49ers quarterback Steve Young had sent his kids to the same Spanish immersion school as our sons, and one of the teachers helped arrange for some of the guys who had worked for the team's security to come to the hotel. Russell interviewed them in our tiny hotel room, a place that was usually meant for business travelers visiting Facebook headquarters. We expanded from one room shared by me, Russell, and the kids to adjoining rooms with the boys on the other side of the wall and the bodyguards next door. "This is fine," I told myself. "We'll order room service. The bodyguards will run interference. We can live here forever and just burn through our nest egg."

Someone—I'm still not sure who—had set up a GoFundMe to help with security costs, but I hadn't even looked at it at that point. I reasoned that we could take out a loan or, worst case, sell our house. We'd figure it out. I was in more of an hour-by-hour state of mind and wasn't even thinking I would have to travel to DC (the bill for that trip would end up being $22,000) and would need to have security measures in place for years to come (the stopwatch is still going on that one).

Only a few people knew where I was staying, and I wasn't planning on having any visitors, but it wasn't long before Carisa showed up. She was bawling her eyes out. Through her tears, she told me her husband had woken her up after reading the *Washington Post* article, announcing, "It's Christine." She had panicked, telling him, "I know the story. She told me years ago. What do I do?"

As Carisa sat beside me, considerably more emotional than I was given the circumstances, it dawned on me that perhaps her reaction was heightened because it was triggered by her own history of sexual assault. I had no way of knowing at the time, but at that moment, women all over the world were also being triggered. The story was sending out shock waves, drumming up a collective reaction that was visceral for every person who had had something similar happen to them.

Carisa was also a caring friend, and she was worried about my safety. But ironically, at least at that time, I'd never felt safer. I had around-the-clock, professionally trained security, who were staying in the hotel room just next door to mine and keeping such a close watch that if I opened my door, theirs swung open immediately. The bodyguards did their jobs *really* well. I didn't think I needed to worry about getting used to their presence, because I figured I just needed to let the news cycle blow over and then we could get back to our normal lives. And I certainly couldn't imagine paying for 24/7 security for more than a few weeks. But damn was it reassuring. I've read that some people actually become addicted to it, and I think I might have, to a certain extent.

As surreal and scary and intense as it all was, I tried to make it seem like a vacation for my sons. Thankfully, they *loved* the bodyguards, who were all ex-military guys, covered in tattoos and so different from the typical people we hung out with. My boys had never seen a gun in person before, and I caught them glancing nervously at the holsters on the bodyguards' hips, but within a few hours, they were convinced that these were the coolest guys on the planet. It was also a lot more impressive to get driven to school and soccer practice by men who looked like they were out of an X-Men movie. And I became the most lenient parent ever, giving them free rein to go to friends' houses for middle-of-the-week sleepovers and to play as much Xbox as their hearts desired.

The perks compensated for the sacrifices, at least for a while. It was strange for them to have kids coming up to them at school, saying, "We know about your mom!" Our hotel was also farther away from their schools, so they had a much longer drive to get there and were often late (which the schools graciously excused them for, given the circumstances). The schools arranged for additional resource officers to be present in addition to our armed bodyguards. The excitement eventually wore off. They missed our dog. They even got sick of the room service food. By Halloween, the youngest would plead, "Can we please go home now?"

That first week of hotel life, though, it all seemed like an absurd short-term experience. When we were in the middle of it, we couldn't see the magnitude of what we had jumped into, much less know how terrified we should have been, especially when we were more protected than we had ever been in our lives. I figured I could just stay in my hotel room with my sweet and fearless security team, playing endless Xbox with my sons and eating room service ice cream sundaes.

However, the Monday after the article came out, Deb appeared on CNN, and when asked if I was willing to testify, she answered, "Yes, yes she is." I didn't see it at the time, but when Keith showed it to me much later, I could almost see Deb swallow a big lump in her throat after she said it. Then I found out that Michael Bromwich, a lawyer with congressional-hearing experience who had represented former FBI deputy director Andrew McCabe after he was fired by the Trump administration, had stepped up to join my team. He had to resign from his firm to represent me, pro bono, which I thought was a pretty badass and commendable move. I wasn't previously familiar with him, but as I googled him, I realized he was more of an insider than anyone I'd worked with so far. Friends were texting me saying,

"I saw on TV you have a new lawyer?" And I'd respond, "Yes! Haven't met him or talked to him, but I love him already."

My legal team kept expanding, adding on a political adviser who flew out to train me to testify. "That seems like a waste of time," I argued, "because I'm not testifying."

"Just listen to her and see if she has any good ideas," my lawyers told me.

I met her in a large home office in downtown Palo Alto, where the owner told me to help myself to anything in the fridge. I'd been living in a hotel, subsisting off cheeseburgers and fries, so I looked in the fridge and grabbed a beer.

The legal consultant was a sharply dressed blonde woman who opened the conversation by listing disclosures of all the clients she'd previously worked with, in order to be transparent about any potential conflict of interest. I figured since she wasn't wasting any time, neither would I.

"I'm so sorry," I said. "I don't know who told you that I would fly to DC to testify, but I'm not. I'm not doing what Anita Hill did. We're going a different route."

Meanwhile, my lawyers were at that very moment working on preparing me to testify. They kept suggesting I just come to DC to talk about "next steps." But clearly, they'd flown this woman out for a good reason. She must have thought I was either a liar or a fool.

"Well, Christine, I just want you to be prepared in case you do testify," she said. "It's what everyone in your position does. We run through every single question you might be asked, especially the uncomfortable or invasive ones, so that you can answer in the best possible way. It's like basic training before any important interview. The process is called murder boards."

That confirmed it. I told her I would absolutely not be doing anything called murder boards.

A lot of people ask me why I chose not to participate in this part of the process. And I have plenty of regrets about how everything played out, but forgoing murder boards is not one of them. Perhaps I would have been more polished. Perhaps I would have been less freaked out. But I'm sure the outcome would have been the same. I didn't need to go through it twice.

IT HAD BEEN five days since my name went public, and I was now meeting with the security team multiple times a day to go over what we could or couldn't do and how we would get safely to any places we needed to go. Suddenly, Palo Alto felt as expansive as Los Angeles because even if we were only traveling two miles as the crow flies, we had to drive circuitous routes in case we were being followed. To go somewhere that would have normally taken ten minutes could sometimes take an hour.

One of my newest legal advisers, Barry, was in town, and we made plans to get dinner in San Francisco, which meant I would need to leave my compound at the hotel. My friend Deepa was heading into the city for an Ed Sheeran concert the same evening, so I figured she could give me a ride. I told my bodyguards like it was no big deal, saying I'd be back in a few hours. They looked at me quizzically and ended up following Deepa's car as she drove me, which was silly and made me realize they could have just taken me in the first place.

I met Barry at a fancy restaurant in San Francisco's South Park neighborhood, and while we were eating, I told him I'd been getting strange calls from people using voice-changing devices and siren sound effects, all saying the same things: variations on how they were going to kill me. I let him listen to one of the messages.

"Let me contact my friends at the FBI," he said. "We can meet with them. What are you doing tomorrow?"

"Um, hiding?" I responded.

The next day, I had a bodyguard drive me back into San Francisco, where Barry and I met with two FBI agents, including one named Anastasia, which I thought was a great FBI agent name. She would continue to be my go-to contact for all the future threats that came into my work, my home, and any institutions I was connected to.

We had to switch up where we were staying yet again, so we moved to an upscale place on Sand Hill Road in Menlo Park called the Rosewood, which offered a two-bedroom house that was nicer than any place I'd stayed on vacation. "It was a bad idea to put me here," I thought as I got comfortable in my new room. "Now I definitely don't want to leave to go to DC." The new place had a pool, which I couldn't use but could at least see from the window of my room. It was certainly better than the view of the construction site I'd had at the previous hotel. Best of all, there was a new room service menu.

My LAWYERS HAD talked to Keith, Carisa, and Rebecca and had a list of additional corroborators I'd told, so now it was time to move on to other areas. Namely, they wanted to find other women who'd had similar experiences with Brett. They talked about it like it was a logical treasure hunt: if they could find other women (because there are *always* other women), we'd have a much stronger case. The first time I heard someone say, "Hopefully there are other women," I was stunned.

"Hopefully there are *not* other women who have gone through this, you mean?" I asked, sure that they'd gotten their words twisted and weren't wishing into existence other victims of trauma. But they were just so focused on the cause—on helping me—that they'd lost sight of the human cost behind what could be beneficial for the case.

I had to admit that I kind of knew how that felt. In my professional life, I worked as the statistician on studies that dealt with trauma survivors and people who suffered from depression and anxiety. It was my job to check the validity of the methods used, interpret the data, and make sure the findings were presented accurately. If my collaborators on the project were hoping for a certain result and the data went their way, I of course felt happy for them. But inherent in those successes were the many individuals who had suffered.

I wondered how this kind of mindset had affected my relationship to my own trauma, perhaps creating an emotional distance from it that had allowed me to keep it from bubbling up to the surface as I studied other people's suffering. Had it helped or harmed me? How would it serve me in this next stage of my life? How would I feel if other women ended up coming forward?

Not long after, my lawyers would relay the "good" news that had come in the form of an alert from the *New Yorker*: a new allegation of sexual misconduct, this time from Kavanaugh's college days.

With that revelation, there were more and more discussions about me going to DC. I had to have someone come to my hotel room to remove the remaining blue dye from my hair so I would present as professionally as possible. I was terrified of testifying and of having to board a plane to do so but reassured myself with the idea that I could just take the next incremental step and make my final decision when I got there. Every flight of my adult life had been a scary one, but that would be one for the books.

Flight Risk

My first encounters with a fear of flying were merely observational, as I watched my dad prepare for business trips. He didn't have to travel often, but when he did, he got much more irritable. My mom would explain to my brothers and me that our dad was just stressed out about work, but my dad was typically a confident and successful businessman. I saw that he only seemed to be on edge about work when air travel was involved. He'd joke about it, mocking how the pilots would announce during the flight, "We'll be experiencing a little chop up ahead," before the entire plane got bounced around by a thunderstorm. But there was something under the surface of his wisecracks. It was ingrained in me early on that flying was something to be apprehensive about.

My dad didn't talk about it much, but he did tell me once that the fear gets better as you get older (I've experienced the opposite, though these days I have access to better medication). I still think of my dad when the pilot comes on over the intercom to say, "We have some slightly unsettled air coming up in the next few minutes." I look around the cabin, marveling at the passengers who barely even notice the announcement or who seem annoyed that he interrupted their movie, while I grip my armrests and prepare for death. I think of my dad when my family members grumble about me being prickly and whisper to each other, "She's flying in a few days."

Of course, just because you have a fear of flying doesn't mean you can avoid ever getting on a plane. Once I moved to California, cross-country flights became more frequent, but they never got easier. However, the farther away I got from my hometown, the more comfortable I became—it just took facing my greatest fear to get there. When I moved another 2,500 miles to the west for an internship at the University of Hawaii, I landed exhausted from six hours of terror and never wanted to leave.

One day while in Hawaii I met a pilot who, when I told him I hated flying, asked me, "You want to go up with me?"

I told him I would rather go snorkeling in the Mauna Loa volcano.

"I do the mail drop for Lanai and Molokai twice a week," he said. "The flight is like fifteen minutes. By the time we get up to altitude, it's time to go down. And it's gorgeous. I bet I can change your mind about flying."

I agreed, but I still almost pulled the emergency alarm once we got up in the air. Then he turned to me and said, "You want to steer?"

I looked at him like he'd asked if I wanted to blindfold him and take tequila shots.

"It might be good for you," he said. "You'll see what's involved. Be in control."

Apparently, he had caught me on the right day. I took the

steering wheel and looked at the monitor, which showed a horizontal line running across the middle of the screen. If you're under the line, that means the nose of the plane is dipping down, and if you're over it, the nose is pointing up, so you just try to stay right on the line. I didn't land the plane myself—or do anything, really—but by the time we were back on the runway, I had nearly decided I wanted to abandon my PhD program in psychology in its final months and become a pilot (only for Hawaiian Airlines, and only interisland flights, of course). Anytime I was on a flight after that, I would try to tune into the channel where you can listen to the flight crew communicating with the airport. I'd be able to hear them talking about turbulence before the pilot even announced it to the rest of the passengers and know that they had already redirected the flight path. I realized that awareness of the practicalities was a great panacea for the fear.

A combination of CBT (cognitive behavioral therapy) techniques, the ability to change my thoughts around flying, and the exposure therapy that happened when I flew the plane—one of the most efficacious treatments for flight phobias, it turns out—lasted about eight months before it wore off.

Thankfully, one of the psychiatrists I worked with early in my career told me, "I can get you something for that." Medication definitely helped, at least with the physiological response—the racing heart, the sweaty palms. I didn't lose the awareness that I was trapped in a plane with no way to escape, but the thoughts were less bothersome.

That said, I don't go out of my way to fly, so when I was getting pressured to go to DC to testify, I was set against it. I let them know the destinations I was willing to travel to: Los

Angeles, San Francisco, San Diego. Maybe Phoenix, Portland, or Seattle, but I'd prefer to stay in California. Otherwise, I figured senators who were more mobile and wealthier than I was could travel to me. I was under the mistaken belief that I had information they would travel for.

Chuck Grassley offered to send some of his staff, including his aide, out to do a full interview. To me, that felt like performing more of the same exercises in futility we'd been doing for weeks. They'd probably meet with me and report back, "Okay, we interviewed her. It's nothing. Just like all the other allegations." Their team would cross it off the list and call it a day. If I wasn't meeting with the senators who were on the committee, what was the point?

I wrote back, saying that if they sent out a couple of senators, maybe one from each party, I would be happy to do a full interview. They replied that they were willing to send aides from both sides of the aisle, ignoring the fact that that wasn't what I had asked for. They kept acting like I was being difficult by asking for senators to meet with me, telling my lawyers that I was in no position to make demands. But I wasn't going to play a game of telephone. Talking about the experience was uncomfortable, and I wasn't eager to lay it all out in detail for people who weren't directly involved. I wanted to tell it to just a few people—the right people—and only once.

My lawyers kept negotiating and telling me to come to DC and we'd figure it out from there. There was so much pressure to just testify already. There was also a lot of pressure *not* to testify. Friends were asking me, "You sure you want to do this, Christine?"

It wasn't really about me *wanting* to do anything, though.

The wave was coming for me—I might as well ride it. On Sunday, September 23, I officially agreed to go to DC, and they set my testimony for that Thursday. Some Palo Alto tech hotshots offered to provide a private plane. There was no paddling back to shore now.

Love/Hate

"My lawyers told me to ask if you think testifying might be therapeutic," I said to my therapist.

She let out a muffled laugh before stopping herself.

"Therapeutic? Talking about your trauma in a public forum and getting questioned? Please remember you don't owe anyone anything, Christine." My boss had used the *exact* same phrase. "I don't owe anyone anything, I don't owe anyone anything." I tried saying it to myself, but it wasn't sinking in or even making sense to me. Do we really not owe anything to anyone? Didn't I owe this to everyone in the country?

I ordered a refill of my prescription for antianxiety medication so I could manage the flight to DC. The online response to my name going public had continued to spiral, with my friends forwarding misleading articles and fake profiles posing as me on Facebook and Twitter. They'd ask if I wanted to report them, but I was busy enough just trying to keep my seventh grader and tenth grader away from the news. If there had been just one or two fake accounts, I might have put the energy into taking them down, but there were so many popping up every day,

I couldn't focus my efforts there. It was like having a leak in my roof: if it had been one continual drip, it would've driven me crazy, but this was as if I had opened my door to find my whole house flooded, and I had no choice but to just walk away.

I had expected some backlash from people who knew and loved Brett. I had prepared myself to cut ties with people I'd grown up with, to avoid going anywhere in the DC area where I would run into people in his circle. I had figured we just wouldn't go to my parents' country club. I thought maybe someone might call me a bitch or a liar, but I could handle that. I had no idea of the scale of the hate that would be directed toward me.

But the other side of the coin was the support that was flooding in. The same day that I decided I would go to DC to testify, Carisa organized a candlelight vigil held in Palo Alto, with hundreds of people in attendance. My coworkers and students went, my friend Kirsten spoke, and it was featured on local news that night. I saw people holding signs that read "Stay Strong Christine" and "We Stand with Christine" while they chanted, "We are her. She is us." A plane flew overhead with a banner proclaiming, "We Believe You Christine Blasey Ford." The sign in front of the local shopping mall was changed to say, "We Believe."

I thought of Carisa and the deep understanding we'd shared when I'd told her about what had happened to me, the way she'd shown up at my hotel with such concern, the fact that this was clearly stirring something deep within her. I could see my situation taking on symbolic meaning for women all over the country, but a lot of the talk around feminism and the #MeToo movement and my relation to it made me nervous. I felt like an imposter because I hadn't been fighting on the front (or even back) lines. Even worse, it felt like if they knew the real me, they'd take it all back. For the majority of my life, I'd hung out mostly with guys. I'd gotten my foot in the door to surfing by having the right boyfriend. Most of the people I was closest to in my social circle and at work were men (this has since changed radically). I was more comfortable talking about sports than women's rights. People were calling me a new feminist icon, but I'd look at my Spotify playlists and see all male musicians, some even a bit misogynistic. I worried that people would eventually find out that I was not the advocate for women's rights they'd made me out to be and I'd get raked over the coals.

Then there were the survivors thanking me for coming forward, saying it inspired them to share their own stories of sexual assault and rape. In comparison to some of their horrific experiences, I felt like mine was not as serious. Or maybe they just showed me how much worse it could have been. There's no Richter scale of abuse that you can place yourself on, but I felt like I was at both ends of the spectrum at once: the representative for sexual assault victims and also one of the lucky ones.

Tree of Life

Between conference calls with lawyers and security updates that left me more bewildered than before, I looked out my hotel window at a tree by the pool, my only view of the outside world. I had always felt like I didn't belong in the DC world and was now feeling like a fish out of water in this circle of lawyers and activists. There had only been one place I'd ever felt that I truly belonged: the ocean. I desperately wished I could go surfing, just sit on my board and drag my hands through the kelp.

I've often said my favorite thing in the world is kelp. Most people avoid it, creeped out by the slippery tendrils that pull at your legs in the water. But to me, it's this perfect, slimy, living thing. Sure, when it washes up on the beach, rotting and buzzing with flies, it's kind of gross. But when you swim out far enough to reach the kelp that is still attached to the ocean floor, you can see why people call it the tree of the sea, with its underwater forests swaying in the tides.

It's not actually a tree, or an animal, or even a plant. It's an organism called a heterokont, in the algae family, and it's the secret to an ocean's health. Kelp forests are the key to biodiversity, supporting a vast array of species. It's no coincidence that Monterey Bay, which includes one of the largest kelp forests, is also one of the most biodiverse ecosystems in the world.

But they can be wiped out by something as tiny and innocuous as sea urchins. Sea urchins eat the kelp, sucking it in rapidly through their bivalves, and are an invasive species that strips the ocean of rich nutrients. Otters tend to keep sea urchins in check, but when the otters' population dips, the urchins can proliferate like crazy. Someone once told me that the water in the Mediterranean is so blue because the ocean floor is covered in sea urchins. It results in gorgeous crystal-clear water but far less biodiversity beneath the surface.

As a surfer, you can get tangled up in the kelp, especially at low tide. When you're paddling through the tips of the kelp "trees," your fin can easily get caught, bringing your board to a quick halt and launching you off into the water. But in higher tides, when there's more room for each strand to drift around, you can use the kelp as a rope to pull yourself faster.

The same thing that can pull you back can also move you forward. I'd just have to hope for high tide.

PART
THREE

Riding the Wave

Deb told me I could bring a small group of people with me for support on the flight to DC. Russell and I decided he would stay in California with the kids and their bodyguards so they could continue going to school. That left friends and colleagues to fill the seven or eight spots.

Choosing the people for my team reminded me of fantasy football. I love fantasy football. As I thought about who would make the cut, I decided I needed people who wouldn't spook me any more than I already was. I also needed to factor in who could miss work and be away from their kids for two or three days. Unfortunately, that meant my friends Tanya, Agustina, and Carisa were out. Carisa came by the hotel to say goodbye and cried as I asked for her help with my kids should they have any questions or need to talk. My friend Jay, whom I teasingly called Smiling Jay because he was perpetually straight-faced, got a spot on the plane. Kirsten, with her nerves of steel and mother-of-four stoicism, was an obvious choice. Keith would be a calming presence, running interference for me and taking care of the others so I wouldn't end up doing that. My friend Chris was generally unflappable, so he got a spot. I invited my colleague Bruce, who had supported me through so many career and life transitions, and my coworker Allison, and I found out that one of my mentors, El Jefe, would already be in DC on business. Whether I decided I could go through with testifying or not, I felt this group would be undramatic and unconditionally supportive.

I didn't know that I should have had my family, not just my friends, in the front row for my testimony, as Brett would during his. No one told me that my credibility would be questioned because my parents weren't there backing me up. I was fifty-one years old, but it felt like people kept asking me to put my parents on the phone. I hadn't had my parents present when I defended my PhD dissertation, so I certainly didn't think they had to vouch for me now. I hadn't lived under their roof for a few decades. Besides, I would be stressed enough without wondering if my mom and dad were comfortable in their seats or hearing my kids shout "Mom!" when I walked in.

There was also the fact that my dad had made it clear that he thought testifying was a bad idea. I saw him as a "Reagan Republican" who was against Big Government (but who was philosophically a Democrat when you drilled down on social issues), so it made sense to me why he was not thrilled about me throwing myself into a government-run hearing. As a conservative who distrusted the media, he was stressed about me becoming a headline news item. He told me, "They've got you in a squeeze," reasoning that a proper FBI investigation would be more likely if I didn't testify—and if I did, it would be derailed. I hadn't asked him or my mom to travel to see me or help in any way—the truth is that I hardly talked to them during this time, I was so wrapped up in the chaos right in front of me. I also didn't ask my parents to speak out on my behalf, knowing that many of their friends and the people in their community might be on Brett's side. Russell had asked his family to make a statement, which they did. I was very grateful for their support. My sisters-in-law spoke on NPR and CNN, while my side of the family remained silent. I hadn't expected anything more, and with my mom's health issues, it seemed logical if not disappointing that they would stay out of it.

When we arrived in DC, I was ushered to my hotel room as my friends took off on the tourist circuit to see the Lincoln Memorial and other historical sights, texting me beautiful photos and lots of comments about the humidity. I was staying at the Watergate Hotel, two doors down from the room that was used the night of the infamous 1972 break-in. The security was so tight that if I opened my door, several other doors immediately opened. Throughout my stay, I ate all my meals in my room, and if I had to leave for any reason, a bodyguard would walk me down a back stairwell that was clearly not meant for guests and desperately needed to be hosed down.

The morning after my arrival, my entire legal team welcomed me with huge smiles and hugs. I loved seeing everyone all together, including Larry and Barry, my eclectic little legal family. I was also grateful that I'd requested a day to rest after getting to DC. I'm sure some people thought I was just drawing things out or delaying the process, but the truth is that I needed that day to allow the medication from my flight to wear off. Even though I always took the minimum dosage needed, I certainly didn't want there to be a trace of it in my system when I testified. What if it gave me the same laissez-faire attitude it granted me when I flew? I imagined myself saying to the committee, "No worries, it's no big deal."

It was a huge deal. After all, besides Anita's testimony decades earlier, this was pretty unprecedented, especially considering the political climate at the time. The only people who had testified in front of the committee under the Trump administration had been Trump's former lawyer Michael Cohen, the former FBI director James Comey, and the former FBI deputy director Andrew McCabe. I wished I could speak with them, especially Andrew McCabe, who had been the last person to testify before me. (I would eventually get to talk with him, and we shared a bond over the retaliation we each experienced before, during, and after our testimonies. Andrew wrote a book about his experience, *The Threat*, and without his perspective, you might not be reading this book. He showed me it was possible to be a whistleblower and talk about powerful people and politicized issues in a fair way.)

Understandably, my lawyers wanted to spend all day prepping me, especially since I'd forgone the murder board sessions in Palo Alto. Part of the negotiations stipulated that I was not to be informed of any of the questions in advance. So they started walking me through the things I *might* be asked. It was both more stressful and less. How do you study for a test that you don't know the content of?

I drove my team up the wall, constantly asking, "Why do we need to worry about that?" and "Why would someone want to do that?" and "Why can't we just be honest and nice?" It seemed as if my lawyers were coaching me to avoid any appearance of fallibility, as if being human was a risk. I felt like the most important thing was to be honest. I didn't think I needed strategy.

Though I would later be described as naive, I think the more accurate word is *idealistic*. I'd grown up believing in the political process. I thought that if the people on the committee had taken this very esteemed job in public service, they wanted to do the right thing.

I clung to that belief because if you can't have hope that there's at least some good in these people, if you can't get yourself to believe that they want to do the right thing for the country, you just don't get off the beach in Santa Cruz.

Do No Harm

Leland and I had been in the same middle and high school friend group. She had closer friends who'd attended Holton since third grade with her, but we hung out together during summers because our families belonged to the same country club. Our bond was based on laughter and memories as middle schoolers hanging out at the country club pool and golf course and later in high school going to parties and dances with our other classmates. She was a little bit older and wiser than me and I looked up to her like a big sister, cheering on her athletic and social bravery.

Perhaps if I'd been older or less insecure, I would have confided in Leland about what had happened in that room with Brett and Mark. But that would have been new territory for us, far more serious than smoking cigarettes on the golf course and praying our parents wouldn't find out.

Leland had been a quintessential Holton-Arms student, with her blonde hair, preppy wardrobe, and promising future. She had always been assertive and confident, and she was a gifted athlete at everything she tried: basketball, field hockey, tennis, and especially golf. Once we graduated high school, we kept in touch, and I visited her at University of Virginia our freshman year, doing the typical partying that kids do when they've escaped a disciplined environment. She went on to become a professional golfer after college and coached at Georgetown, until chronic pain ended her career.

After I moved to California, Leland and I mostly lost touch, and I had only seen her a few times in the last twenty-five years. I'd heard through the grapevine that she wasn't doing well, dealing with both her chronic pain and addiction issues that I believe resulted from her pain medications.

I WAS CERTAIN I hadn't told Leland what had happened that night with Brett and Mark, but I sent her a private message on Facebook on the July day that Brett was nominated. I didn't get a response until weeks later, when she wrote back simply, "Yikes!" That confirmed it for me: "Keep Leland out of this. She is in no place to help." Other people would prod me, saying, "You never know; she might remember something?" But I didn't want to jeopardize her health by getting her mixed up in all of this.

After the *Washington Post* article was published, Leland wrote to tell me she was so proud, that she along with her ex-husband (now close friend) wanted to help, and that I could go on their podcast to make statements. She said I needed a local DC attorney and offered PR genius and former governor of Mississippi Haley Barbour. Not having left the hotel room in two days, and spending most of my time among armed security, her generosity and connection were just what I needed. We talked briefly on the phone, reminiscing about the times we'd spent driving around in her mom's old station wagon, meeting up with boys. She recalled that we had liked those Prep boys, and she said, "Then didn't we figure out they were losers?" For a moment, it felt a little like we were teenagers again. It reminded me of the times we'd spent scheming together over how to get invited to a party. When she offered to give me a statement of support, it felt like she was saying she could give an alibi to my parents so we could stay out all night.

I thanked her and told her that I had plenty of people helping, that she should just take care of herself. The next day, she told me she was ill and her ex-husband was running interference. She was "working on getting gone" and said that hiding was the best strategy. A slew of media was outside her door. I felt terrible and helpless but she reassured me over text that she was going to send me a safe number and signed off, "You're my hero!" I wondered if I would hear from her again.

Four days later, before traveling to DC, her name popped up on my phone and I smiled to see "I love you and I'm really proud of you. I wish I could be more supportive and that my statement was more helpful. I'm really ill and need medical attention so I had my lawyer do it. I'm sorry if I let you down." She had not let me down and I assured her I understood. I would forge on. She continued to send uplifting messages conveying her and her daughters' support. In quiet moments, the guilt pulled at me. I hadn't helped Leland with her podcast and I had not helped as much as other classmates with her recovery struggles. I hoped the stress the situation was putting her through would end soon.

Testimony Eve

My lawyers handed me a statement they'd prepared for me to read in front of the committee and gave me a pen for any notes I wanted to make. As I read, I started crossing out line after line. I labored over each phrase, every detail. I'd make my notes, they'd type up a fresh copy and print it out, and I'd go through it again, adding just as many red marks as before. Mark up, print, read, and repeat.

When I worked on research papers, I entered a kind of flow state, putting each statement under the microscope to make sure it was presented accurately. After weeks of feeling out of my element, I was finally in the zone. I thought about the lawyers, the senators, the reporters who would be in the room when I spoke. They would all just be doing their jobs. If they could treat it like work, I would too. I decided to testify like I taught and to prepare my statement like I authored the studies I worked on: ruthlessly committed to the data.

In science, you present information without bias, to a panel of your peers. But as I spent more time with my lawyers, I learned that bias and partisanship had far more influence than the information on the table. I was fascinated by the stark difference between science and law. "That's a weird way to get at the truth," I thought. "The better argument wins?"

Larry and Mike walked me through a litany of dos and don'ts, and I took notes at a long conference table in the Watergate. While appreciative of the guidance, some of their tips seemed a little obvious: Don't answer a question you don't know the answer to. Don't add unnecessary details. No offense to them, but I was trying to recall an otherwise ordinary night from thirty-six years ago—I couldn't add superfluous details if I tried.

At one point, Larry looked at me with a grave face and said, "Christine, I just want you to know that if you cry, that would be all right." "It's okay to cry," I scribbled. It may sound like common sense now, but at the time I was grateful for being told specifics and reassured that I could be myself. After we'd gone through the brief preparation, Larry leaned toward me across the table and gave me the best advice I could have received.

"Just remember, if you can walk in that door, you've already won."

Something stirred in me, competitiveness edging out the dread for one blissful moment.

"They don't want you to even show up," he continued. "They've been doing everything they can to scare you away, to silence you. So the moment you sit in that chair, you've won."

That was enough to get me to finish tinkering with my statement.

But there was one more thing to figure out: what to wear. I had shown up in DC in a Billabong hoodie, cropped jeans I'd had for fifteen years, and some teal sandals. But I'd brought a small selection of the professional clothes I taught in—mostly shift dresses and cardigans. I never put a lot of thought into shopping for my day job, usually choosing whatever I could find at Nordstrom Rack that came in my size and was comfortable to teach in for long lectures. I wore dresses for the simple fact that they were easier, an entire outfit in one piece, so I had just one decision to make. As I'd gotten older, I cared less about what I wore, and it was freeing. Some days I'd teach in a band T-shirt.

When it came time to decide on my outfit for the testimony, the team in DC didn't even look at what I'd brought, saying, "Don't worry about it. We'll go to Saks Fifth Avenue and choose something for you." Toward the end of the day, a rack of clothes rolled in, what looked like ten versions of the same outfit, all sets of matching black blazers and black skirts. It was as if I were the most boring cartoon character of all time. I already didn't like making decisions, and having to choose between a bunch of cloned versions of a Washington, DC, uniform felt like a joke.

Upon closer inspection, one had a larger collar, and one had a little ruffle on the sleeve. I thought about my red shift dress hanging in the closet and decided not to bring it up. Then I noticed that one of the suits was navy blue. The color of the ocean.

"I want the navy one," I said.

They took all the other ones away and presented me with a pair of Prada heels. I took a photo and texted it to a colleague who always teased me about how casually I dressed (I didn't realize I would later get an $800 bill for the suit and a $200 bill for the shoes). I briefly tried on the suit and heels. Not a perfect fit but definitely better than what I'd brought. "I'll be sitting down the whole time anyway," I thought. Besides, what was important was presenting the data. I decided to go to bed as early as possible to be rested and ready.

I went to bed at nine and woke up at midnight.

I was going to need some coffee.

A Credible Witness

Getting my hair and makeup done in my hotel room made me feel like I was getting ready for a wedding. When we arrived at the Senate office building where the testimony would take place, I told myself cold feet were to be expected. My lawyers walked me down the aisle, like an extremely weird wedding processional. Politicians filled each doorway in the hallway leading to the courtroom, staring and smiling at me like wedding guests. Perhaps my navy suit counted as my "something blue."

My lawyer Deb would later tell stories about me looking like a deer in the headlights at that moment, asking, "This isn't going to be on TV, right?" The truth is, they had told me it had to be videotaped for other senators to view—but they didn't tell me it would be televised until we were walking down the hall. I no longer had the option to fear the camera, so I just told myself it was C-SPAN on a workday, and no one I knew watched C-SPAN at work. I was mostly just trying to make sure I got one foot in front of the other without falling. (I should have practiced walking in the heels—they were much too big.) Finally, I got to the end of the hallway and entered the hearing room, staying close to my bodyguard. I settled into my chair and arranged my notes on the table. A wisp of hair kept falling in front of my eyes. I looked up at the huge United States seal, an inspiration and a threat. This was so much bigger than me, or him, or any of us. It made me shrink a little in my seat. But then I thought of what Larry had said. I had made it to the chair. I'd already won.

Chuck Grassley started the proceedings. He lamented that both Brett and I had been through a terrible couple of weeks. He mentioned Brett's long record of service, saying that the FBI had just done its sixth background check on him since 1993 and had never found any incidences of inappropriate sexual behavior. He made jabs at Dianne Feinstein for keeping my letter a secret. He said that his staff had made repeated requests to interview me (failing to mention that he'd refused to interview me himself or send any actual senators to do so). He explained that during my cross-examination, the Republican senators would be using a prosecutor who worked on sex crime cases to handle questioning on their side (instead of having an all-male panel poke holes in the story of a sexual assault victim—not a good look).

There was an undeniable edge to Grassley's voice throughout, as he threw in emphasis ("My staff made eight requests, yes, *eight requests*, for evidence"), mentioned "stonewalling" from attorneys, and brought up the fact that Leland had said in her statement that she didn't remember attending a party with Brett. By the time he passed it over to Feinstein, I was ready to crawl into a hole. Feinstein briefly addressed Grassley's claims about her handling of the letter and its confidentiality before shifting her focus to me.

"In the meantime, good morning, Dr. Ford. Thank you for coming forward and being willing to share your story with us. I know this wasn't easy for you. But before you get to your testimony, and the chairman chose not to do this, I think it's important to make sure you're properly introduced—"

Grassley cut in. "By the way, I was going to introduce her, but if you want to introduce her, I'll be glad to have you do that. But I want you to know, I didn't forget to do it, because I would do that just as she was about to speak."

Feinstein continued: "Thank you. I have to say, when I saw your CV, I was extremely impressed. You have a bachelor's degree from the University of North Carolina–Chapel Hill; two master's degrees, one from Stanford and one from Pepperdine; and a PhD from the University of Southern California, better known to Senator Harris and I as USC. You are a professor affiliated with both Stanford University and Palo Alto University. You have published over sixty-five peer-reviewed articles and have received numerous awards for your work and research."

No one had told me that they would introduce me by going through my résumé. Yet here was Dianne Feinstein listing my accomplishments, suggesting that I had the kind of background that made me credible. What if I hadn't graduated college? What if I was still a cocktail waitress? How would they have introduced me in that case? Realistically, I probably never would have been offered a chance to testify.

By the time it was my turn to speak, I was sweating. But then I reminded myself again that I'd made it to the chair. Just like I'd managed to put one foot in front of the other in my much-too-big Prada heels, I would put one word in front of the other.

"I am here today not because I want to be. I am terrified. I am here because I believe it is my civic duty to tell you what happened to me while Brett Kavanaugh and I were in high school."

The committee members looked down on me from their raised platform. I glanced at Chuck Grassley, hoping for an unlikely source of reassurance despite his harsh opening statements, since we'd had a pleasant and cordial conversation before the testimony. He'd stopped by my room to introduce himself and was so hard of hearing he'd had to turn his head so that his good ear was facing me when I spoke. He had told me that he would see what he could do to make this fair but that it would be quite hard. I was still in the mindset of believing in the process, so I said, "Thank you so much. I almost went to Iowa State for graduate school. Such a beautiful state." Some of my team of advisers and friends were silent but likely cringing—why was I being so nice to him? I sensed that in their stalwart work on my behalf they'd had some really tough conversations with him. In my mind, we were going to be working for two hours together, and I'd be sharing my deeply personal and painful experience with him, so there was no reason to be unkind (even though he might have leaked my information to the press and ignored my requests to do things privately). I just tried to be a real person with him, and in the moment it felt like he had returned the favor. It was actually a really nice exchange, and oddly, it put me at ease. I thought, "If I can have this conversation with him, I might be able to really do this." I tried to keep that in mind as I told my story for what felt like the first, and four hundredth, time.

"I do not remember all of the details of how that gathering came together, but like many that summer, it was almost surely a spur-of-the-moment gathering. I truly wish I could provide detailed answers to all of the questions that have been and will be asked about how I got to the party, where it took place, and so forth. I don't have all the answers, and I don't remember as much as I would like to. But the details about that night that bring me here today are ones I will never forget. They have been seared into my memory and have haunted me episodically as an adult."

Below me in some sort of terrifying orchestra pit, countless photographers lay down as if on the savanna waiting to capture a photo of an elusive lion. I'd been told there would be one camera, but the shutters were clicking faster than the court stenographer's typing. It was overwhelming, but I had no option but to keep it together, even when they all jumped up at once and snapped away from every angle. (Some extreme fringe news outlets would catch me with a crazy expression on my face, while others would photoshop me to look ten years younger. I would never recognize myself in any photo from that day.)

"When I got to the small gathering, people were drinking beer in a small living room on the first floor of the house. I drank one beer that evening. Brett and Mark were visibly drunk. Early in the evening, I went up a narrow set of stairs leading from the living room to a second floor to use the bathroom. When I got to the top of the stairs, I was pushed from behind into a bedroom. I couldn't see who pushed me. Brett and Mark came into the bedroom and locked the door behind them."

I avoided the camera lenses and looked back up toward the committee members. There was Orrin Hatch, the elderly senator from Utah who I had wanted to help as I watched him slowly and carefully enter the dais above me with the help of a walker and who, after my testimony, put out a statement saying

I was "attractive," which people on both sides of the political aisle deemed inappropriate or called a poor choice of words. He later amended it to "pleasing." I reminded myself that the people in front of me were human beings, and forged on.

"I was pushed onto the bed, and Brett got on top of me. He began running his hands over my body and grinding his hips into me. I yelled, hoping someone downstairs might hear me, and tried to get away from him, but his weight was heavy. Brett groped me and tried to take off my clothes. He had a hard time because he was so drunk and because I was wearing a one-piece bathing suit under my clothes. I believed he was going to rape me. I tried to yell for help. When I did, Brett put his hand over my mouth to stop me from screaming. This was what terrified me the most and has had the most lasting impact on my life. It was hard for me to breathe, and I thought that Brett was accidentally going to kill me."

I looked over at Dianne Feinstein. She had come to say hello to me before the testimony as well but had made me feel more nervous because she seemed shaky and edgy herself. I glanced over at Lindsey Graham, who refused to look at me. All of the other senators made eye contact with me, and the ones who weren't allowed to speak to me—except Graham—gave me at least a gentleman's nod, briefly tilting their head downward. (In surfing, the same greeting is a slight nod upward.) Senator Ben Sasse even came by to say hello to me at one point, surprising everyone since I had been told that no Republican senators would speak directly to me, only through the lawyer they'd hired to question me. Senator Graham, however, often stared up at the ceiling throughout the hearing.

"During this assault, Mark came over and jumped on the bed

twice while Brett was on top of me. The last time he did this, we toppled over, and Brett was no longer on top of me. I was able to get up and run out of the room. Directly across from the bedroom was a small bathroom. I ran inside the bathroom and locked the door. I heard Brett and Mark leave the bedroom laughing and loudly walk down the narrow stairs, pinballing off the walls on the way down. I waited, and when I did not hear them come back up the stairs, I left the bathroom, ran down the stairs, through the living room, and left the house."

I had my hand on my lawyer Michael's knee. In any other context, it would have been extremely inappropriate. But I really needed someone to hold my hand, and he didn't offer his, so I just clutched his leg. There was a great deal of emotion in my voice, which I guess is why most people assumed I was reliving the trauma of what had happened that night during my testimony, when in reality I was sitting there telling the most personal story of my life to people I didn't know, intimidated by the grandeur of the US Senate and the authority in the room. It was beyond strange, and it was about to get stranger.

"As the hearing date got closer, I struggled with a terrible choice: Do I share the facts with the Senate and put myself and my family in the public spotlight? Or do I preserve our privacy and allow the Senate to make its decision on Mr. Kavanaugh's nomination without knowing the full truth about his past behavior? The sense of duty that motivated me to reach out confidentially to the *Washington Post*, Representative Eshoo's office, and Senator Feinstein's office was always there, but my fears of the consequences of speaking out started to increase."

I shifted in my seat. The feeling in the room was tense and uncomfortable, even though all everyone else had to do was listen. I thought about what El Jefe had told me: there are some things you just have to do alone.

"My greatest fears have been realized—and the reality has been far worse than what I expected. My family and I have been the target of constant harassment and death threats. I have been called the most vile and hateful names imaginable. These messages, while far fewer than the expressions of support, have been terrifying to receive and have rocked me to my core. People have posted my personal information on the internet. This has resulted in additional emails, calls, and threats. My family and I were forced to move out of our home. Since September 16, my family and I have been living in various secure locales, with guards. This past Tuesday evening, my work email account was hacked, and messages were sent out supposedly recanting my description of the sexual assault."

Apparently, I was doing a good enough job. I didn't know it at the time, but twenty million people were watching, and even Fox News was calling me a credible witness. I wouldn't be able to watch my testimony until four years later, and it would still be intolerable then. But every year going forward, I would know exactly what had happened on each day from June through October, and I would relive it all, day by day. "Today is the anniversary of the polygraph test," I'd note to myself. "Today is the day I talked to Dianne Feinstein." And, of course, "Today is the testimony day." I can't stay in bed for four months out of the year, but sometimes I want to.

"Apart from the assault itself, these last couple of weeks have been the hardest of my life. I have had to relive my trauma in front of the entire world and have seen my life picked apart by people on television, in the media, and in this body who have never met me or spoken with me. I have been accused of acting out of partisan political motives. Those who say that do not know me. I am a fiercely independent person, and I am no one's pawn. My motivation in coming forward was to provide the facts about how Mr. Kavanaugh's actions have damaged my life, so that you can take that into serious consideration as you make your decision about how to proceed. It is not my responsibility to determine whether Mr. Kavanaugh deserves to sit on the Supreme Court. My responsibility is to tell the truth."

"I did it," I thought. "Hardest part is over."

After I read my statement, Rachel Mitchell, the prosecutor the GOP had hired to question me, began her cross-examination.

"I just wanted to tell you the first thing that struck me from your statement this morning was that you were terrified," she said. "And I just wanted to let you know, I'm very sorry. That's not right."

"How nice of her," I thought. "Maybe this won't be so bad."

From there, the questioning was broken into choppy five-minute segments. For five minutes, a Democratic senator would thank me for my courage or send barbed comments toward the Republican side and call for a proper FBI investigation. Then Rachel Mitchell, as a stand-in for the Republican senators, would interrogate me. During the first round, she asked me some preliminary questions for clarification before Chuck Grassley interrupted and moved the questioning along to Dianne Feinstein, whom I'd already told the details to in our phone call weeks ago. I imagined this would be a similar rehashing. Instead, Feinstein asked me why I'd held on to this information all these years and how I could be sure it was Brett who attacked me.

"The same way that I'm sure that I'm talking to you right now, just basic memory functions," I told Feinstein. "And also just the level of norepinephrine and epinephrin in the brain that sort of, as you know, encodes that neurotransmitter, encodes memories into the hippocampus. And so the trauma-related experience then is kind of locked there, whereas other details kind of drift."

Earlier that morning, I'd had breakfast with El Jefe. In an effort to distract me from the day ahead, he'd asked about some data analyses I was working on. Eventually the conversation turned to what they might ask at the hearing.

"They're not going to ask me how memory actually works, are they?" I wondered, presenting it as both a very real and ridiculous possibility.

"What would you say?" he asked.

"Imagine if I went into a whole thing on cortisol and memory encoding," I mused.

We had chatted about the duality of memory, how traumatic moments can imprint themselves on your brain permanently while also obscuring details. It was too scary to talk about the death threats, the behind-the-scenes manipulation, the complete and utter lack of control I had in the situation. So we talked about what we knew: the circuitry of the brain, the science behind this crazy situation. I didn't expect to break it down for Dianne Feinstein right out of the gate. But I'm also grateful I'd had that breakfast, because otherwise who knows how I would have answered the question of how I could trust my memory.

The questioning went back to Mitchell, who asked me if

I'd had anything to drink the day of the party or if I'd been on medication at the time. The tone shifted. Mitchell started asking me about my fear of flying. I was confused, wondering, "Aren't we going to get back to the part where I'm trying to help you guys?" I had all these notes in front of me. Didn't they want to see the medical records from when I'd told my therapist about this? Or the list of people I'd told over the years before my name was leaked? Or anything that was actually relevant?

Instead, Mitchell kept poking holes in my assertion about being afraid to fly, pointing out that I'd flown frequently for work and gone on vacations to faraway destinations. I understand now that she was implying that if I could fabricate a phobia, I'd be capable of lying about other things as well. Later I would have one of those mock conversations you have after the fact, when you come up with a better answer you wish you'd said in the moment. With the benefit of hindsight, and with debilitating adrenaline no longer coursing through my veins, I would respond in my head weeks later, "You can be afraid to fly and still fly because you have to. As many as 40 percent of people on any given flight are fearful to some extent."

Instead of having that kind of wherewithal in the moment, I answered Mitchell's challenges factually, staying myself, and before I knew it, she seemed to have made her point and moved on.

Later, Mitchell asked me, "Was it communicated to you by your counsel or someone else that the committee had asked to interview you and that they offered to come out to California to do so?"

I turned and addressed Chuck Grassley directly, deviating from the protocol.

"Can I say something to you?" I asked. "Do you mind if I say something to you directly?"

"Yeah," Grassley replied stiffly. My lawyers shot glances at each other, clearly uncomfortable with me going rogue.

"I just appreciate that you did offer that," I said. "I wasn't clear on what the offer was. If you were going to come out to see me, I would have happily hosted you and been happy to speak with you out there. It wasn't clear to me that that was the case."

It was my one moment of pettiness. To everyone else, it seemed like an exchange of pleasantries over a fumbled meeting, but secretly, I was calling Grassley out on the fact that he had never really offered to come to California to meet with me. I wanted to mess with him a bit, knowing that it wouldn't change anything but that it would at least give me a tiny bit of pleasure.

We moved on from the topic, but Grassley came back to it, saying he appreciated me acknowledging that they'd said they would come to California.

"You and I both know the truth," I thought.

When it was Vermont senator Patrick Leahy's turn, he addressed Grassley, saying, "Chairman, you and I were both here twenty-seven years ago. At that time, the Senate failed Anita Hill. I said, I believed her. But I'm concerned that we're doing a lot less for these three women today. That's my personal view. Now Dr. Ford, no matter what happens with this hearing today, no matter what happens with this nomination, I know, and I hear from so many in my own state of Vermont, there are millions of victims and survivors out there who've been inspired by your courage. I am."

He addressed the potential of mistaken identity, and I confirmed that there was no way I would mix up Brett or Mark with somebody else. Then Leahy said, "Let's go back to the incident. What is the strongest memory you have? The strongest memory of the incident, something that you cannot forget. Take whatever time you need."

I didn't need much time to formulate my answer.

"Indelible in the hippocampus is the laughter. The uproarious laughter between the two, and their having fun at my expense."

"You've never forgotten that laughter," Leahy responded. "You've never forgotten them laughing at you."

Leahy went on: "Dr. Ford has at times been criticized for what she doesn't remember from thirty-six years ago. But we have numerous experts, including a study by the US Army Military Police School Behavior Sciences Education, that lapses of memory are wholly consistent with severe trauma and stress of assault."

It went back to Mitchell, questioning me on behalf of Lindsey Graham. She challenged what I'd said about how many people were there and whether I could hear the conversation downstairs as I hid in the bathroom after the attack. At some point a map of my old neighborhood was brought out to challenge how I'd gotten home from the party.

Finally, we took a break, and as I sat in my little holding room, someone showed me a photo from Pearl Jam's Instagram account. It was a picture of me being sworn in, with the caption "A Patriot." I can't imagine that they knew I was one of their biggest fans. It was the boost I needed to get back out there.

We returned to the hearing room, and the rest of the questioning devolved into a tennis match between Democrats criticizing the way the nomination had been handled and Chuck Grassley stepping in to defend and deflect. On the sidelines was Mitchell, trying her best to get in the game and dissect my statements. I kept expecting my lawyers to jump in and object when the hearing turned into a weird interrogation of my character. Wasn't that how it happened on TV?

But every time I turned to my right to look at Deb, she looked straight ahead, only interrupting once to clarify who had paid for my polygraph test. She would later tell me that as I fielded questions about seemingly everything other than my attack, she was looking at the faces of the Republicans and thinking, "They really believe her. What are they going to do?" She couldn't communicate that to me in the moment, though, so she and Mike just kept pushing my notes in front of me, as if there were some unspoken rule that I was the only one at the table allowed to talk.

I felt fatigue washing over me. Thankfully, along with Larry's crucial counsel, Mike had given me the advice to just tune out whenever the committee wasn't directly addressing me. It became a survival technique that I clung to as the cross-examination went on. There was a lot of cross talk, so I used that time as a necessary mental break. When the questioning turned back to me, I exerted all of my effort to listen carefully, paying attention to every word and choosing my own with the most consideration I could muster. But whenever the bickering between parties picked up, I switched back into preservation mode.

Finally, after four head-spinning hours, it was over. Chuck Grassley thanked me for my bravery, and Rachel Mitchell shook my hand and said, "I will pray for your safety," which sent chills down my spine. I stood up and finally saw my colleagues and the handful of friends who had been sitting behind me the entire time. I was used to seeing them in their bathing suits, not business casual. "They really spiffed up for this!" I thought while I was patted on the back and told "good job."

As I left the room, my brain felt like it had been scooped out with a spoon. I had no interest in watching or even hearing about Brett's testimony. "He's a judge," I thought. "It'll probably go a lot more routinely than mine did."

I Intend No Ill Will

Early on, when my friends and I were still bantering back and forth at the beach and then the pool, I thought there was a possibility that Brett Kavanaugh would step down to avoid putting his family through an investigation or further scrutiny. "Save us both the trouble," I wanted to say to him. "I don't want this as much as you don't want this." But I never expected him to reach out to me and try to right his wrongs.

I've been asked, "What would you have done if he reached out and apologized?" I don't even know how to begin to answer that. Who would he be apologizing to—me? The country? What would he be apologizing for—that night? The harassment around the testimony?

All I can guess is that if he'd come to me, really leveled with me, and said, "I don't remember this happening, but it might have, and I'm so sorry," it might have been a significant, therapeutic moment for survivors in general, and in that whole moral quandary over whether this was the only bad thing he'd ever done, I might've wobbled a bit. I might have thought,

"You know what, he was a jackass in high school, but now he's not."

But when my story came out and he flat-out denied any possibility of every single thing I said, it did alleviate a little of my guilt. For me, the question of whether he had changed was answered. Any misgivings about him being a good person went away.

The fact is, he was there in the room with me that night in 1982. And I believe he knows what happened. Even if it's hazy from the alcohol, I believe he must know. Once he categorically denied my allegations as well as any bad behavior from his past during a Fox News interview, I felt more certainty than ever that after my experience with him, he had not gone on to become the consummately honest person befitting a Supreme Court justice.

That said, I had never, ever wanted his family to suffer. I had asked to keep things private for both our sakes. When my allegations came out publicly, the media started reporting that he was getting threats. It troubled me a lot.

Then I remembered that I'd already had to move to a hotel because of the threats to me and my family. Again and again I thought, "Why is he putting us all through this? Why can't he call these people off? Say something—anything—to condemn the harassment happening on both sides?"

Now I know better. Brett couldn't have called them off, because they were part of a machine much more powerful than he was. From well-funded conservative organizations to fervent extremists, whether with money or through more radical means, some of these people were in a position to control what *he* was doing, not vice versa. He was beholden to the moderate *and* the extremist factions, being forced into a Jekyll and Hyde dynamic depending on the audience. Instead of handling the situation in a consistent, authoritative manner, he oscillated between restrained pleas for "due process" to maintain an air of decency and then references to Clinton conspiracies and political hit jobs to stoke the flames of the Far Right.

I've heard many people say, "Imagine if your character was being called into question in front of the entire country after decades of public service." I get that. But shouldn't a thorough review of your entire history be part of the process for a job interview at that level? If you can't handle that, then maybe you're not qualified for the job.

I would later read Chanel Miller's memoir, *Know My Name*, in which she describes her experience in the aftermath of a sexual assault on the Stanford campus in Palo Alto—the same case I'd discussed with my friend Keith when my own sexual assault was nothing more than a terrible memory and not yet a major news story. Describing the process of pressing charges against her rapist, who was a Stanford athlete at the time, Miller writes, "When a victim does go for help, she is seen as attacking the assailant. These are separate; seeking aid is her primary motive, his fallout is a secondary effect. But we are taught, if you speak, something bad happens to him. You will be blamed for every job he doesn't get, every game he doesn't play. . . . Each time a survivor resurfaced, people were quick to say what does she want, why did it take her so long. . . . Why don't we ask her how it was possible she lived with that hurt for so long, ask who taught her to never uncover it."

People also ask me, "Do you think you ruined his life?" Despite the fact that Brett ultimately got the job. Despite the fact that he sits on the Supreme Court while I still receive death threats, pay sky-high security costs, and continue to live a very limited version of the life I had pre-testimony. My response to questions like that is usually, "I think it was probably hard on everyone's family." Because that's what I still feel bad about.

MUCH HAS BEEN said about Brett's testimony, which directly followed mine. The red face, the screaming, the inappropriate jabs at Democratic senators, the infamous declaration "I still like beer." There's not much I can add. Regardless of how you feel, only one of us was testifying as a candidate for a lifelong appointment to one of the most prestigious jobs in the world. I'd held to the field trip rules I'd been taught as a child about how to behave in the Senate. He had not.

Over time, I would see short snippets of Brett's statement and questioning, and the anger on his face imprinted on me forever. He was enraged, his face twisted into an angry glare, words spewing from his mouth like venom. Some took it as justified fury over being wrongfully accused. Others thought he intentionally turned up the volume on the vitriol to make up for being more even-keeled in previous interviews and statements. He needed to put on a show for Trump and the radically conservative folks who were judging him from afar, wondering if he could adequately push their agenda.

While I had shunned murder boards and extensive prep for my testimony, I was told Brett had an entire team of people preparing him. I suppose we were similar in viewing it as a work event, though; because Brett actually worked in this world, he seemed to know that strategy and performance were the most important factors. He knew to put his wife and daughters front and center, while I had balked at the idea of staging my family as extras in the production. I didn't know that my integrity was on the stand as much as Brett's.

The day of our testimonies, the *Washington Post* ran an article with the headline "Christine Blasey Ford's Family Has Been Nearly Silent amid Outpouring of Support." It mentioned a letter that had been signed by a dozen people from my family, but none of them had been my parents or brothers—they were all from Russell's family. My in-laws wrote a heartwarming statement and called me a woman of impeccable character, and Russell's mom told reporters, "All I can tell you is that we love her. She has been a wonderful parent and an upstanding citizen, and I'm happy to have her as a daughter-in-law." My sisters-in-law were interviewed on national news to show their support. My immediate family's silence highlighted the immense love coming from friends, cousins, nieces, aunts, lifelong colleagues, and strangers across the world. We don't get to choose how others respond when we are in crisis, but I am grateful for people who stepped in like family.

After several attempts, the reporters writing the piece were finally able to reach my dad, who gave the following statement: "I think all of the Blasey family would support her. I think her record stands for itself. Her schooling, her jobs and so on. I think any father would have love for his daughter."

I was surprised he even engaged with the media as we had talked about simply needing to survive the twenty-four-hour news cycle. I knew others thought his statement was not good enough. I noticed it was indirectly phrased, in contrast to the way he usually speaks. Sure, I saw what they meant, but knowing my family and having talked to a few of them over the course of the summer, I truly wasn't surprised. I had been telling myself for two months that I could do this alone. It wasn't worth any points their support might've scored me on the believability scale. Besides, even if they had been there, it's not like that would have changed the vote. Pointing to my parents' absence as proof that they didn't support me was just one of many straws to grasp.

I also knew why the media was focusing on it. The fact that my dad belonged to the same golf club as Brett's dad was easy pickings. They played it up like the two were close friends who hung out all the time, which wasn't true. But it was too juicy an angle: the story of an elitist raising his kids in the Beltway and then his daughter going rogue and crashing the Good Ol' Boys Club that he's a part of. I get that there's a satisfying irony for some people in the idea of my dad doing everything he can to place his family in this hoity-toity bubble and then me turning around and bursting it.

The truth is that my dad *is* a bit elitist. He enjoys places that describe themselves as exclusive. He came from a generation in which the American dream was something you could still aspire to. After getting into a fair amount of trouble at school, he joined the army and turned his life around. He went from working as a roof tarrer to working his way up the chain at a bank to owning his own business and sending his three kids to college without ever having a degree himself. And look at the results of the decisions he made and the way he raised me and my brothers: all three of us have loving families, graduate degrees, and successful careers.

For all the difficult parts of my upbringing, I stand behind my dad and appreciate his intentions. In a way, even though I left the Beltway, I'm raising my sons the way he raised me. We live in Palo Alto so they can attend top-tier schools. I push them to participate in sports, and I'm perhaps a little overly invested in their schooling. I don't make them play golf—even though, ironically, they enjoy it—but surfing is nonnegotiable in our family. I'm more aware of the drawbacks that come with growing up in an elitist community, so I try to balance it out by spending summers in Santa Cruz and exposing them to other cultures. But it's just a West Coast version of wanting the best for my family, like my dad wanted for his.

The thing about my dad is that he's *my dad*. To everyone else, he became a symbol, something they could twist and turn to their liking so they could say, "Even her own father didn't come out and say he believed her." But I understood. And I thought it was more important for me to protect my eighty-three-year-old dad than for my dad to protect me. Unfortunately, that headline is not as good for clickbait.

I DIDN'T WANT to hear Brett testify. I'd heard everything I needed to hear when he denied the allegations after the *Washington Post* article. At the Watergate after my testimony, I asked to turn off the TV so I could avoid the play-by-play. But I could still glance over and see it in an adjoining room, like a party guest I was trying to avoid. At one point, someone who had been watching said, "I don't think it's going very well."

He called the confirmation hearing process a "national disgrace," likening it to a search-and-destroy mission. He described the effort to block his nomination as a "calculated and orchestrated political hit," suggesting that he had become the victim of a left-wing revenge plot that had been fueled by a Trump presidency. He ominously cautioned that "what comes around goes around."

Then he addressed the allegations by mentioning that one of his closest friends is a woman who was sexually abused. He said his mom had overcome workplace sexual harassment as a lawyer. He pointed to the fact that he had always had a lot of close female friends, rattling off a few by name—"Amy or Julie or Kristin or Karen or Suzanne or Maura or Megan or Nicki"— and adding that "several of those great women are in the seats right behind me today." Two of them had introduced me to Brett and his friends when we were in high school.

He stated, "I never attended a gathering like the one Dr. Ford describes in her allegation." Later he presented calendars that showed his daily activities, including numerous house parties during which he said he and his friends drank beer.

He brought up Leland a few times, pointing out that she didn't remember the party in question (leaving out the fact that she said that even though she didn't remember it, she believed me). He said that all the people I alleged were there agreed that it hadn't happened (though in fact no one said it hadn't happened—they all just stated that they couldn't recall it). This wasn't surprising or conclusive; after all, trying to remember a casual get-together that happened thirty-six years ago on a night that wasn't remarkable in any way (unless you were sexually assaulted) is an understandably difficult thing to do.

When asked about his drinking, Brett didn't answer directly and instead described his academic record. He repeatedly denied being a heavy drinker or ever blacking out. Yearbook entries showed that he was the treasurer of the "Keg City Club," and multiple people who knew him throughout high school and college would later attest to seeing him wasted, slurring, and completely incoherent.

At one point, Brett turned the questioning of his drinking habits around, warning, "If every American who drinks beer or every American who drank beer in high school is suddenly presumed guilty of sexual assault, we'll be [in] an ugly new place in this country."

Brett scoffed at the fact that a Supreme Court hearing would bring up high school yearbook entries and pose questions about getting drunk. As if the senators were the ones who'd written about "boofing" and "Devil's Triangle" and referred to being an "alumnus" of a female classmate, a joke among Brett and fellow football players that was meant to suggest they'd all had sexual relations with her.

The question wasn't whether partying and acting crudely as a teenager disqualified Brett from being on the Supreme Court. It was whether he could be truthful about it. To me, his suitability for the job should have been made clear in his response to the charges. Brett's response was to clap back with rage and, I am convinced, lie under oath.

Chanel Miller wrote in *Know My Name*, "Why is it that we're wary of victims making false accusations, but rarely consider how many men have blatantly lied about, downplayed, or manipulated others to cover their own actions?"

The week of the testimony, *Saturday Night Live* parodied Brett, bringing in Matt Damon to portray him with a dead-on impersonation of the excessive sniffling, shouting, and emotional outbursts about everything from his school buddies to his beloved beer. People kept sending me links to it, asking if I'd watched it, saying that it was the funniest thing they'd ever seen and that Damon's performance was perfect. I couldn't bring myself to watch it. I wasn't ready to laugh about it.

Brett had said in his testimony, "I intend no ill will to Dr. Ford and her family." I would think about that in the year that followed as his friends made my life hell. He told a story about one of his daughters saying to his wife, "We should pray for the woman." I needed more than prayers at this point.

Zombie

As a small group of friends, family, and my legal team gathered in a suite on the top level of the Watergate overlooking the Potomac, I tried to collect myself. My crew from Palo Alto were there, as were a few friends from high school. My parents and my brother's wife walked in. I was surprised—it was nearly my parents' bedtime, and I hadn't thought my mom would be up for an event like this. Ever since she'd had a stroke a couple of years previously, all of us had treated her pretty delicately. My dad went around shaking the hands of my friends (he would text me the next day telling me how proud he and my mom were and how nice it was to meet my California friends), while my mom walked over to me and gave me a hug and a kiss. I wasn't quite sure how much she had been made aware of.

"I saw you," she said slowly. "I saw that you didn't like when people said nice things about you. You've been that way since you were little."

I was blown away. The person I thought might not be able to even absorb the testimony picked up on something that no one else could: who I'd always been, despite the moves, despite the degrees, despite everything. While everyone else was congratulating me on being so composed and compelling, my mom saw me squirming when Mazie Hirono and Cory Booker called me a hero. She saw me look away uncomfortably when they were reading my résumé. While everyone else watched Christine Blasey Ford testify, my mom saw Chrissy.

I WOKE UP the next morning feeling cognitively impaired, as if I'd been drugged. I could barely string words together. The highlighter I'd taken to my thoughts and memories, and the care I'd taken to present the data—it was all gone.

Breakfast was brought in, and I ate my bacon, eggs, and toast with my bodyguard. Then Deb called and asked me to come downstairs so that I could say hello to someone she really wanted me to meet. I said I was not presentable and was even more exhausted than last night, but she promised it would be quick. After finishing my meal, I was led down a back stairwell that stank of cigarettes, urine, and rotten eggs.

I was brought into a conference room, where Deb sat with another woman. I didn't recognize the other woman—she certainly wasn't the cool and mellow Lisa who I was used to seeing at Deb's side—but immediately noted that she was put together impeccably, with sharp eyes and a warm smile. "Do I know her?" I wondered, thrown off by the familiarity she projected. I looked down at what I was wearing—jeans and flip-flops. Whatever this meeting was, I was utterly unprepared for it. Then I realized with horror that I was still very much cognitively and physically incapacitated. I knew my name; I knew I was in DC. But beyond that, I'd hit the wall. It was as if the last three months of living off adrenaline and stress had finally caught up with me.

Deb introduced me to the woman, acting like I was supposed to know who she was when she told me her name. It reminded me of when my kids talked about their favorite rappers and I pretended to follow along. I finally put together that the woman was a reporter for the *New York Times*.

"Nice to meet you," I managed to squeak out—sheer autopilot response. The woman launched into an excited monologue that, in my hazy state, sounded like the voices of the adults in Charlie Brown: "Whah whah whah such a good job whah whah best testimony whah whah whah writing a book whah whah #MeToo whah whah whah whah whah now it's going to be about you."

I looked blankly at Deb, shrinking into my chair.

"You're going to be in a book—can you believe it?" Deb said, smiling with pride. She was beaming and talking quickly. Our energy levels could not have been more different.

I'm not sure why anyone would have thought that on that morning—of all mornings—I'd want to meet with anyone. But I knew Deb really wanted me to meet her.

I nodded my way through the rest of the meeting, not wanting to be rude but mostly wanting to do whatever it took to get out of that room and on my way home—well, not technically home, but to the next hotel. I had never looked forward to a flight in my life, but I couldn't wait to leave this experience behind forever.

As soon as I got on the plane, I felt—irony of all ironies—safe. As we took off, I looked out the window, imagining that geography was all it would take to whisk me away from this entire situation. Like the night I'd gotten home from that party in high school, I felt a weird sense of relief. I'd managed to escape relatively unscathed. Sure, some terrible things had happened, but I'd gotten out alive. I'd be able to move on now.

A Man's Life Is Shattered

After my testimony, polls showed that most people believed I was telling the truth. Even Trump called me a credible witness and a "very fine woman." Celebrities were reaching out left and right to offer support. Survivors were posting emotional tributes on social media, saying, "Your story is my story." People were writing to tell me that I'd inspired them to speak out about their own sexual abuse and assault. I was too tired to take it all in, but I was being told the impact my testimony had made. I still felt like a zombie, but a decent zombie who had at least tried to do the right thing. That lasted about three days before the real character assassination began.

Apparently, most people in similar situations—whatever those may be—get torn apart immediately. I would be told later that the time it took for the opposition to drag me down was a sign of how well I had done. It was a blessing and a curse—I'd done so well that they had to work even harder to sit with it and really figure out their game plan before they went on the attack. Because they believed me. Because most people believed me.

News stories were flooding in and getting forwarded to me

what felt like every minute. A couple were incredibly flattering. As a scientist, the tiny factual errors bugged me. I could see it, the riptide where the truth and narrative were mixing, creating a building current. Overnight, the small but noticeable divide between truth and news turned into a gulf. With articles appearing across hundreds of news outlets and social media, different stories were being created along political party lines along with endless conspiracy theories. My confidence in myself and our country's leaders up and drifted away.

On October 2, just a few days before the vote, Trump mocked me at a rally in Mississippi. He made fun of me for not remembering certain details of the night in question, saying, "How did you get home? I don't remember. How'd you get there? I don't remember. Where is the place? I don't remember. How many years ago was it? I don't know," with a crowd of smiling fans behind him laughing and clapping at his impersonations of me being cross-examined. Gone were his initial descriptions of me as a "good witness." Now he was saying, "A man's life is in tatters. A man's life is shattered."

I wasn't angry, because it was more bizarre than infuriating. A month ago, no one beyond my social circle had known who I was. How was I *supposed* to react to now being mocked by the United States President on national television? It was almost validating in a very messed-up way because if I hadn't done a good job, maybe Trump wouldn't have even held the rally. Like many others, he had believed me, so now he had to do something to discredit me. I wasn't happy that the president was ridiculing me on a worldwide stage, but I was still feeling bolstered by all the positive messages I'd received, so it felt more surreal than shattering.

Others saw it for what it was: horrendous, inappropriate, and unpresidential. Mazie Hirono, the senator from Hawaii, spoke about Trump's behavior, saying, "We can always count on the president to go down to the lowest common denominator—mock people, call them names, attack them." Responding to Trump's assertion that it's "a very scary time for young men in America," she said, "They must think that we all sit around making up stories about them. We have a few other things that we like to do, such as getting on with our lives and making a living." She explained that responses like Trump's are part of the reason that sexual assault survivors do not come forward. She later added, "Sexual assault survivors often don't remember 'how many steps,' 'how many rooms,' the kinds of things the president mocked Dr. Ford about. But they remember the attack itself with 100 percent accuracy."

Jeff Flake, the Republican senator from Arizona, called Trump's comments "kind of appalling," adding that "to discuss something this sensitive at a political rally is just not right." Flake had come in to say hello to me in my little holding room after the testimony—something that was highly unexpected and that boosted my spirits. He had looked like he was going to be sick. I quickly tried to make my expression more somber, as just a minute earlier I'd been warmly embraced by Mazie Hirono and we'd joked about how I wanted to be one of her Hawaiian constituents. Now facing the opposite feeling with Flake, I didn't know what to say, so I offered, "If you have any questions you want to ask me, if you want to know anything else, I can meet with you." It was so awkward. Everyone on my team looked on silently.

But I really appreciated the gesture on his part. I admired the courage to show his face.

Strangely enough, because the leader of the United States openly mocked me and generated threats that went all the way to the FBI, I now qualify for political asylum. One could say I became sort of an enemy of the state in my own country. But I can't just pick up my kids and move our problems to Canada or New Zealand.

Regardless, I certainly wasn't in a position to consider fleeing the country when the death threats ramped up as a result of Trump's mockery. A lot of people checked in with me after the rally, offering messages of horror and shock and anger. But my mind was elsewhere. Something had happened the same day that rattled me much more.

My legal and crisis teams called me before the Trump rally and asked, "Who is Brian?" My heart sank. Shit. The ex-boyfriend I didn't call while going down the list.

Weeks earlier, I'd been relieved when a quote from Brian was published in *The Wall Street Journal* before my testimony, saying he'd met me while I was getting my master's at Pepperdine and found me "sweet, cute and with a good attitude." He said he would never do anything to undermine my credibility. It was a surprisingly kind and supportive quote considering we hadn't parted on the most amicable terms and I hadn't heard from him in twenty years, but with all the other things I had to worry about at the time, I welcomed anything that felt like it wasn't directly coming to annihilate me. The news of him was quickly pushed out of my head to make room for all the other terrifying possibilities that lay before me.

But apparently, that wasn't all he had to say. After my testimony, Brian contacted the Judiciary Committee with a written statement, saying that in the nineties when I was a grad student, he had seen me use my psychology training to help a friend prepare for a lie detector test as part of the job interview process for a government position. The friend in question was Tory, my dearest friend from high school, who had also moved to California in our twenties, and remained a loyal pal throughout the testimony process.

Tory made a public statement in response, denying that I— or anyone else—had ever helped her prepare for a polygraph exam. My team issued a statement saying that I stood behind my testimony. It was ludicrous to imagine me coaching anyone for a polygraph, considering the first one I had experience with wouldn't happen until decades later. I was furious that Brian would drag her reputation like that. She was retired by then, but she had dedicated her entire career to public service. She and Brian had remained friendly even after he and I broke up, a fact that caused me a little irritation but no surprise, considering Tory stayed friends with everyone she ever met.

There I sat on the hotel bed, watching the president of the United States openly ridicule me in front of millions of people, but all I could think was, "I can't believe this is happening to Tory."

"You have to fix this," I told my lawyers. They were all so sorry, adding their empathy to the notes and texts from friends and strangers around the world. They assumed I meant the Trump thing, but I was actually talking about Brian. There was more in his statement. He claimed that in the six years we dated, he had never witnessed my fear of flying or discomfort in confined spaces, citing the fact that we'd once traveled around Hawaii in a small plane and that I'd lived in a tiny five-hundred-square-foot apartment.

Brian's letter was enough for Chuck Grassley to demand access to any videos or photos from my polygraph test, my therapy records, and all communications I'd had with Emma Brown, who had written the initial *Washington Post* story that revealed my identity. The Senate Republicans were waving Brian's statement around as proof that I couldn't be trusted. (Apparently this ex-boyfriend from my twenties could be trusted, without any of the scrutiny I'd gone through.) I was just as confused as I was frustrated. Why had he chosen to speak up after saying he would never try to discredit me?

THE NEXT THING I knew, it was being reported that Leland was saying she'd been pressured by people "on my side" to change her initial statement to indicate that she believed me even though she couldn't corroborate my story. And who was reported to be one of the people pressuring her? Tory.

I felt blindsided again. Leland had clearly been stressed out, but even after my testimony, she'd texted me, "Hey, I'm so proud of YOU! You rock, we will keep supporting! Don't give up, don't ever give up & know that you're [*sic*] courage has bled into my courage in fighting this disaster I'm in." What had changed?

While Trump told the Mississippi crowd that a man's life was shattered, I could only think about why Tory's life was being

192 ONE WAY BACK

turned upside down. No one was going after Keith, Carisa, Rebecca, or anyone else with information about me or Brett in the same way. My lawyers suggested that because Tory was a Republican who had worked for the government, she was a much more dangerous person to have on my side. It made sense, they said.

"You guys come from a really messed-up world," I said. "I'm glad I work in health care."

My communications with Leland became more sporadic from there as I guess we both were trying to get our lives back on track. She sent me sympathetic if erratic messages checking in to see if I was okay and letting me know the toll that all of this was taking on her and saying that she didn't understand why everyone left town and wasn't talking to her. I wrote her back and she was elated to hear from me, asking if she could send a card. She apologized for not being more supportive and "needing to have a lawyer do it." She had medical bills and legal bills piling up. I asked how I could help and said that I was so sorry anyone was still bugging her about my situation. She said she was used to being a public person and had been blessed with a savvy media lawyer in addition to her regular lawyer. She promised to visit once she was in better health. Then late one night in April 2019, a message informed me, "I'm $100,000 into your mission of the century."

I HESITATED TO write about Leland. It still doesn't feel right. But leaving her out would mean not telling the whole truth. The media loves to write about our friendship as a case of betrayal, saying that I don't talk about her because I can't explain why she won't corroborate my story. But the truth is that I don't talk about her because I still care about her. I still feel terrible that my situation caused her so much stress and pain in a life that had already seen more than its fair share.

Regaining our connection only to lose it again stung, and stings. But my friendship with Tory was on a deeper level and had continued throughout the decades since high school. She and I had gone through so much together—apartments, boyfriends, graduate school—and nothing had rattled our bond. Suddenly she stopped responding to my calls and texts.

It's surreal to have a person drop out of your life so quickly. Weeks would go by, and then one day we would both be included in a group text between high school friends, and proof of her existence would smack me in the face.

I'd try to talk about it with Russell or other close friends, who would offer useless advice about friendships running their course. One person sent me an article with a headline along the lines of "Some Friendships Aren't Meant to Last." "That's not the case for this relationship," I argued. We didn't just move in different directions, our connection fizzling over time. An outside force came and pummeled us like a tsunami, and instead of clinging to me for safety, she had been forced to let go of me to save herself.

Another friend insinuated that perhaps we were never as good of friends as we thought, and I was hurt at the mere suggestion. Later, I went back and put each year of our friendship under the microscope, trying to look for signs. But all I saw was how much we'd stuck by each other since seventh grade.

The post-testimony retaliation required some geographical moves, damaged my reputation, and spread misinformation that no legal or PR counsel could contain. The retaliation was successful in distancing and dividing me from my friends, family, and students in order to not take any risk with their safety. But all of that pales in comparison to the worst way in which it hurt me: it damaged the friendship that had mattered most to me in the world.

The ugly, painful truth was clear: regardless of whether Tory and I could repair our friendship down the line, we would never be best friends again.

"Upstairs, downstairs, where was it?" Trump said as he parodied the testimony at his rally. "I don't know. But I had one beer! That's the only thing I remember."

In fact, I had given hours of testimony about what I remembered that night, the most unforgettable being the laughter between Brett and Mark as I feared for my life. Now a wall of people laughed as Trump stripped me of my "very fine woman" status, failing to mention the one thing I'd said I was 100 percent sure of: my attacker's identity.

There were a couple of young boys in the crowd cheering behind Trump. They were dressed in little suits and ties. At one point, one of them waved his hand in the air, giving a thumbsdown as Trump described the charges against Kavanaugh.

"How horrible is this?" Trump repeated.

"A man's life is shattered."

Glass Half Full

The one thing that would've helped during this time was something I couldn't do: surf.

I'd flown back to California but had to stay in hiding. I craved the calm of the crashing waves, the overpowering, in-the-moment presence that they require. Some people don't feel safe in the ocean. I didn't feel safe on land.

I would've jumped at the chance to surf even shitty waves, though California is renowned for having some world-class surf spots. While Hawaii has warmer water and solid waves every day of the year, some surfers there still appreciate the smoothness—"glassiness," in surf speak—of California waves. In order to catch the time of day known as "glass off," you need to go about an hour before dark. Between about noon and 7:00 p.m., the wind tends to pick up, blowing off the top of the waves and making for a rough, crappy ride. But when you catch a glassy one, you can just glide down the entire line of it while it slides into shore.

I used to check my phone for surf conditions, but now it buzzed with security alerts. I missed the simple determinations

I used to make in the Before Times: Do I need a new board? Can I fit in a session before lunch? What spot should I go to?

One consideration when deciding where to surf in California is whether you want to ride a beach break or point break. A beach break is when the waves break over a sandbar that runs parallel to the shore, making the waves look like they're being pushed toward the beach by a straight rake. A point break, on the other hand, is when the waves roll in at an angle, sweeping across the beach like a searchlight scanning a prison yard.

A beach break gives you a quick, rough ride, often dumping on you as it plows toward the shore like a heavy carpet unrolling. At a beach break, you must be ever vigilant about the waves, making sure you dive under them as they roll in, while at a point break, you can position yourself out of the diagonal line of the wave and just sit on your board without worrying about waves breaking on top of you.

Unsurprisingly, beach breaks are harder to surf, with faster, shorter waves and a swift drop in. Ocean Beach in San Francisco is a famous beach break that's been kicking surfers' asses for years. Meanwhile, point breaks like Steamers Lane and Pleasure Point in Santa Cruz can send a surfer on a ride the equivalent of ten waves at a beach break. The slow, unfurling crest of the wave can allow you to coast seemingly forever.

You'd be justified in assuming I prefer point breaks, but you'd be wrong. The beauty of a beach break is that you can surf anywhere along the wave, instead of one specific starting point. And perhaps more importantly, beach breaks are far less crowded—there's just so many more waves to work with. I always needed to have my own space. I never wanted to feel trapped while doing the thing I loved the most.

Before finding myself on hotel arrest, I used to head out in the morning, when only a few other surfers dotted the horizon. I usually aimed to surf for an hour or until my arms got tired, whichever came first. I'd catch a wave, and by the time I stood up, it would be over. Paddle out. Pop up. Wipe out. Paddle out. Pop up. Again and again.

Afterward, I'd walk along the beach and pick up sand dollars, throwing them back into the ocean in case seagulls hadn't already eaten the urchin living inside. I imagined their insides filling once again with salty water, given a second chance at life.

The ocean has so often been painted as dangerous, something that could snatch a life and pull it down into its depths. But I know the truth. If you've already been washed up on the shore, it can rescue you. You can get back into the water and survive.

PART
FOUR

The Waiting

After I'd nodded my way through the odd meeting with the *New York Times* reporter the morning after my testimony, my friends and I boarded the plane back to Palo Alto. Drinks were served, but I couldn't bring myself to order anything. I already felt kind of drunk, and not in a good way. I was disoriented, fatigued in every bone of my body.

The whole summer I'd had a purpose. It was such a singular focus, one that came with so much adrenaline that it had given me stamina, clarity. Now, it was as if a wave had come and taken me by surprise, knocking me down and stealing away my resolve as it swept toward the shore. It reminded me of the brutal times I'd gotten pounded by a relentless set, desperately trying to get back up when I'd already exhausted myself. I always told my kids that if they got stuck in waves like that, they should never ever let go of their board. Try to duck dive or turtle roll. In the worst case, just stay on your board, turn it toward the beach, and hold on tight, and the next wave will push you to shore even if it crashes on you. But I had nothing to hold on to anymore. I felt a sense of dread creeping up my spine.

"Hey, guys, listen up," Jay suddenly called out. "Jeff Flake is calling for an investigation!"

He read the news as optimistically as if it were an announcement of a grandchild being born or a major job promotion. My friends seemed buoyed by the update, and even I was tentatively encouraged. "At least that's not terrible news," I thought. I settled into my seat, still exhausted but not as disturbed.

Before I knew it, we were crossing the Sierra Nevada, and as I looked at snowy crests and peaks that resembled sea foam in a churning swell, I felt genuinely relieved. Everything would be fine in California. People were working to investigate further. I'd get to hug Russell and the boys.

Checking back into the same hotel I'd stayed at when I'd first gone into hiding, I marveled at all the progress the construction workers had made on the new Facebook offices. It gave me a weird sense of hope and pride, like a mom seeing her baby walk for the first time. I didn't think to question the strange relationship I'd developed with my quasi prison; in fact, I embraced it. I would text and email friends who checked in and tell them I was "just sitting at home," when actually I was sitting in my hotel room.

Russell, the kids, and I blew through the room service menu, trying to convince ourselves that working our way through each item could be a fun game. But after we tried the customary Caesar salad, spaghetti bolognese, and ice cream sundae, we ended up ordering burgers most of the time. They all tasted the same— dry bun, dry patty, and a lingering smell that made me sad. It was an aroma out of context, meant to waft through the air at a backyard barbecue, not stick to white hotel sheets. The novelty had worn off. My sons missed their dog, their home, their basketball hoop in the driveway.

Our boys continued going to school with their bodyguards, and Russell continued going to work while evading the bodyguards as much as possible. The fall quarter was well underway, but I couldn't teach or even leave my hotel room, given the news that an extended investigation was taking place and that the vote would be postponed. Keeping the safety of me and my students in mind, I was tentatively planning to be available to support the person taking over my teaching duties and to resume research when possible. With the exception of brief trips down to the lobby to eat lunch while my bodyguards sat at a nearby table, I stayed in the hotel room watching the construction going on across the street. It was preferable to watching TV, where I could be ambushed by my own face at any moment. Each wall that went up on the construction site was a sign of progress I could cling to as I waited for the FBI to knock on my hotel room door.

My lawyers had explained that while there was an investigation underway, the FBI would not just show up unannounced—they generally called first. Nevertheless, after sending the boys off to school each morning, I still got dressed and made sure my notes were in order. Sometimes I'd poke my head out the door as if FBI agents had simply gotten lost in the hallway. Each time I opened the door to my room, my security team would open up *their* doors to see what was going on, and my bodyguards would look at me as if I were a toddler they'd put to bed, only to have me appear in the doorway a few minutes later.

"I'm just seeing if they're here," I'd say sheepishly as they nodded and waited for me to slink back into my room. I would reorganize all my paperwork, laying everything out on the shiny, dark table. I had the notes from my therapy sessions in which I'd described the attack years before the nomination. I had the affidavits and list of friends and coworkers I'd told throughout the years, including an officemate I'd said something to five years before the nomination, when I'd looked up the photo of Brett with President George W. Bush. I had text threads proving that I had tried to come forward with the information months before I testified, that it was not some last-ditch effort to foil the nomination, at least on my part. I didn't feel like a zombie anymore. I was ready.

It was supposed to be a one-week investigation, and three days had already passed. "There's an FBI office just up the street," I told myself. "Perhaps they're doing the longer-distance interviews first." Finally, my lawyers called me and said that the investigation was over.

"But they haven't even talked to me," I said, unable to comprehend. "I still have everything here."

"They're not coming," Mike said.

"But they haven't talked to Carisa," I said. "They haven't called Rebecca. They said it would take a week—it's only Tuesday. How can it be over?"

Still halfway expecting someone to knock on the door any minute, I looked again at my medical records and corroboration from multiple practitioners. I felt like keeping it to myself was akin to withholding evidence. I told my lawyers that if the FBI wasn't going to look at the medical records, I'd just release them myself.

"You absolutely cannot do that," one lawyer replied.

I argued back and forth to no avail until my lawyers called on Barry to try to reason with me, knowing he was my favorite person on the legal team. He was a very successful criminal defense attorney, but he spoke like a psychologist, leading with empathy over logic.

"I'm supposed to talk you out of releasing your records," Barry said later that day. "But I'm not going to do that. We are your lawyers. We are supposed to help you do what you want to do. So if you really want to release them, I will help you."

"Thank you," I said, feeling more convinced than ever that Barry was my favorite. "But why are they so against it?"

"You did an incredible job," he said. "You've made a massive impact."

"And that means I should just give up?" I asked. "Quit while I'm ahead?"

"Releasing your records is only going to help people discredit you," he said. "Don't give them another thing to use against you."

"What, that I've been in therapy?" I asked.

"You work in psychology, so you don't see it like a lot of people do," he explained. "Believe me, I know that being in therapy for as long as you have is commendable. But that's not how the general public will view it. They'll just use it to destroy you. You don't need to become the poster child for mental illness, Christine."

"I don't mind being the poster child for mental illness," I said. "If they want to rip me apart for going to therapy, I'm okay with that. If it means that the next person in my shoes doesn't have to go through this, I'll take it."

This whole pseudo-investigation felt ridiculous. Weren't people saying I was crazy anyway? I'd seen some of the headlines and even some memes making fun of me.

Then I thought about all the times I'd heard and read countless strangers telling me, "I believe you." It never felt as empowering as I'm sure people meant for it to be. It was a subtle distinction, but it felt less like confirmation of something that had happened and more like "I don't think you're a liar." As if I'd told someone that I teach statistics and they responded, "I believe you." It isn't exactly affirming. But I was always comforted by their kindness and said thank you. As for the people who didn't believe me, or the FBI investigators who hadn't even interviewed me, I didn't see how sharing the specifics of my therapy history, anxiety, and PTSD would make things any worse.

Barry had told me that if I really wanted to release my records, the legal team would have no choice but to help me. I contacted a colleague at Stanford Medicine to find out about "waiving privilege," which means you undo the confidentiality of medical records. It was not something you could walk back. As I spent a day deliberating what to do, information was coming about who was going to vote for Brett. By Wednesday, it didn't seem like releasing my records would stop the train. It wasn't worth doing further damage to my family, especially my sons, who kept telling me that kids (mostly girls) were running up to them at school to ask, "Was that your mom on TV?" I knew they were proud of me, but I also knew that they would have to continue to shoulder the burden of my public persona.

So I sat and stared at the construction site. I became more and more fascinated with it. As time went on, my mind started to play tricks on me. The building became a Lego set, with tiny men walking across the miniature steel beams, each day blurring together so that the progress looked like a flip book being shuffled. "That is so cool," I thought. "I wish I was a construction worker." Perhaps people were right. Perhaps I was crazy.

Anyway

The vote on whether to confirm Kavanaugh to the Supreme Court was scheduled for Saturday, October 6. Most of the time during any issue going before the Senate Judiciary Committee, Republicans vote with their party, and Democrats with theirs. But this time, it was clear that many of the Republican senators believed me or were dismayed by Brett's conduct during his testimony. Would that have the power to change anyone's vote?

Jeff Flake was the wild card. He'd had the decency to visit me in the holding room after my testimony. He'd called for the FBI investigation. If anyone was in a position to go against the Republican Party, it was him.

But just before the vote, it was announced that Flake would be supporting Brett.

At that very moment, two women, Ana Maria Archila and Maria Gallagher, had been waiting outside Flake's office, along with a CNN crew who had come to try to get an interview with him. Archila was an activist and childhood sexual assault survivor, while Gallagher had never spoken publicly about her own assault but had been compelled to show up and do something to support other survivors. They received the news alerts of Flake's plan to support Kavanaugh, and just moments later, they spotted him hurrying down the hall with some of his staff.

Their interaction with the senator was caught on camera by CNN, as the women charged into the elevator, blocking the doors from closing, and unleashed emotional pleas as Flake's team jabbed the Door Close button.

"You have children in your family," Achila said. "Think about them. I have two children. I cannot imagine that for the next fifty years they will have to have someone in the Supreme Court who has been accused of violating a young girl. What are you doing, sir?"

Gallagher joined in, shouting, "I was sexually assaulted, and nobody believed me. I didn't tell anyone, and you're telling all women that they don't matter, that they should just stay quiet because if they tell you what happened to them, you are going to ignore them. That's what happened to me, and that's what you are telling all women in America, that they don't matter."

Flake looked beyond uncomfortable, unable to ignore—or escape—the women's chastisement. He was a person trapped in a small space with two people blocking the exit. How similar. How different.

He looked down at the elevator floor, which only prompted Gallagher to demand, "Don't look away from me. Look at me and tell me that it doesn't matter what happened to me, that you will let people like that go into the highest court of the land."

This went on for a few minutes before the elevator doors closed and Flake got away without confirming his decision or agreeing to delay the vote. But on news networks for the rest of the day, he remained stuck in that elevator as the scene streamed across screens all over the country. The two women were being commended for their courage—rightly so.

But I knew Republicans. Like my dad, they were all about decorum, civility. Flake had come to my holding room after the testimony because it was the good-mannered thing to do, not because he was a fan of going rogue. So seeing the women confront him like that in the elevator made me nervous. It was an incredibly brave, unorthodox thing to do, and yet I knew that most Republicans did not take kindly to those acting outside the formal etiquette that prevailed in the halls of GOP offices (of course, this was before things like the insurrection at the Capitol and ongoing extremists in Washington). It felt like an act of feminist betrayal to be anything but effusively encouraging of Achila and Gallagher, but the Beltway baby inside me was afraid that Flake and his colleagues would see this as demonstrative of the fanatical left wing.

To be clear, I thought those women did the right thing. I wanted to applaud them for their ability to show the kind of anger and despair I hadn't summoned in myself. But I also worried that it was a risky way to approach someone like Jeff Flake.

I sat in my hotel room and thought about everything that had happened that week. Trump mocking me at the rally: Strike one. An FBI investigation that skirted important interviews and evidence: Strike two. A widening divide between left and right that threatened to overpower truth and justice: Strike three.

Barry advised me to do whatever I could to distance myself from the outcome. I did my best and was too busy to think very deeply about it anyway. After the long week of waiting for the FBI to do their thing, as the vote approached, I was inundated again with emails, phone calls, famous people, reporters. I'd be on a call with my lawyers and have to jump off to help my kid with his homework. Then I'd be reading an important email update, and my security guards would tell me I had a visitor in the lobby. I didn't have the capacity to absorb much advice, much less steel myself for whatever potential rejection or blowback I might receive. I was simply treading water.

In the end, Brett was confirmed in a 50 to 48 vote while I watched college football in my hotel room. Senator Lisa Murkowski of Alaska was the only Republican to not vote in support of his confirmation, saying, "I believe Brett Kavanaugh's a good man. It just may be that in my view he's not the right man for the court at this time."

The outcome wasn't really a surprise. But the justifications for it still felt contradictory. Most people believed me, but he got the job anyway. The committee said no further corroboration had been found, but had they really looked for further corroboration if they hadn't even interviewed the existing corroborators? Or, for that matter, me?

A theory of mistaken identity had emerged, led by the White House lawyer who had viewed my LinkedIn profile, claiming that I had mistaken Brett for his friend Chris, who I had briefly dated (and thus could accurately and easily recognize). I issued a statement refuting the claim after thinking Brett would make a statement to look out for his friend. Even though Chris wasn't at the get-together and they do not look or act alike, the theory was convenient and couldn't be disproved. As a fifteen-year-old

I had never thought that decades after the fact I would need to gather concrete proof that this had happened. There weren't any eyewitnesses beyond Mark Judge. And Leland couldn't remember that particular evening, which was understandable. I couldn't be absolutely certain that Brett remembered it, but I felt in my gut that he did.

Senator Mazie Hirono and I would speak about the mistaken identity theory a few months later when I visited Hawaii and went to her office to thank her for her support. We talked about the data that showed survivors rarely mistake their attackers. In my field, that would be associated with delusional disorder, a diagnosis so rare that even my colleagues have only seen it a few times on dramatic television.

Regardless, I was told that even if I had medical records describing the assault and identifying Brett as the attacker, as well as twenty people saying they'd been told about it years earlier, an actual videotape of him doing it would not have made a difference. Even with that video, they could have denied it was Brett on the footage. All told, belief in my story essentially amounted to "thoughts and prayers."

I thought of Anita Hill, who had eyewitnesses who were never interviewed. I thought of the people who had called what Brett had gone through unfair, a disgrace to the legal system, but didn't seem to have a problem with an incomplete FBI investigation.

Everyone was texting me broken-heart emojis. "At least you all are safe now." "Can you go home?" "Can we have dinner?" "Imagine if he didn't get the job!" My dad sent me a text message about how in every battle there are casualties. I felt misunderstood by everyone on the planet.

Needing to do something other than spend the rest of my life watching college football, I started my own investigation, conducted through taking screenshots on my phone and compiling all possible documents that would at least keep the US historical records accurate. I had thousands of text messages, emails, and corroborative statements that could show that my story was not a last-minute effort to block Kavanaugh's confirmation. I just needed to gather the data.

My quasi investigation forced me to go back and look at all my communications over the last few months. I was struck by the chasm between the way I'd felt during each moment and the politeness I'd hidden behind. Even in the aftermath of the Feinstein breakup letter, after I'd snapped on the phone call with my lawyers, my responses were all variations of "Yes, I understand. Thanks for your help." I was not, as so many articles were referring to me as, "a badass." I'd been a good girl who followed the rules, and look where it had gotten me. Perhaps I should have been more like those women in the elevator with Flake.

However, while I stewed in regret over everything I'd done in the lead-up to testifying, I never questioned my conduct during the testimony. I knew that the way I'd presented the information, about the experience itself and the long-term effects, had helped survivors feel seen. I knew that the ultimate outcome was not a result of something I'd done wrong during the dizzying hours I spent in front of the Senate Judiciary Committee. It was a result of what was wrong with the people who had heard it, who had heard him, and decided to disregard me and give him the job anyway.

I would learn two years later that more than 4,500 tips

about Kavanaugh were submitted to the FBI's tip line. A portion were sent to Trump's Office of White House Counsel, and the remainder went uninvestigated. Trump also determined which people the FBI interviewed during their investigation, which made it clear why they never got in touch with me. Democratic Rhode Island senator Sheldon Whitehouse would post on Twitter after this came to light, "Here's a thought: nothing prevented Trump White House from using FBI tip line information to direct FBI investigation *away* from percipient or corroborating witnesses."

Ever since the vote, lawyers have been coming up to me and telling me that if I had been their client, it would have gone the other way. Or that if my case had been put in front of an actual jury, I would have won the day. But of course my case hadn't been heard in a real court. It was almost a mock trial. What does winning even mean in that case?

I don't fault my lawyers in the slightest, and I will always be grateful to them. They were the first ones willing to represent me. They didn't charge me. In fact, they spent their own money. They still stand behind me. I don't think they ever did anything that they thought would harm me; they advised me to the best of their knowledge. I was not an easy client, and handling my psychological meltdown the year after the testimony was not part of their job description. They may not have wanted Brett on the court for many reasons, but they mainly tried to help me come forward to tell my truth. They didn't think the consequences would be as bad as they ended up being. No one did.

The only silver lining of Brett's confirmation was that my family and I wouldn't have to worry about people coming after me to avenge Brett's failure to get the job. As soon as Russell heard the news, he told me we didn't need four bodyguards anymore. Even the security team confirmed that according to their assessment, the threat level had gone down. There were still people contacting me saying they wanted to kill me, but we were safer.

Hibernation

We moved to another new location, this time a house in the northern part of Palo Alto. It was probably only a ten-minute drive from our own house, but I felt like it was three hours away. I swapped my construction-site view for a view of a tree, this time measuring my days in terms of how the leaves on the branches had changed. Russell went to our house to get our bedding so we would feel more at home, and he bought me a fuzzy gray Ugg blanket. He knew it would cheer me up—it was the same brand as the boots that my students at Stanford wore to class and that surfers wore after changing out of their wet suits on cold Santa Cruz mornings. I'd owned three pairs since grad school.

The gray blanket became an extension of me as I sat on the bed all day, with the dog we'd been reunited with snoozing next to me and my sons playing NBA2K on the TV. I went from over-parenting to feeling like I was doing zero parenting. Other people would pick my kids up to go to practice, then drop them off. It was my Gray Blanket era: a noun *and* a verb, and I planned to Gray Blanket and wait until it all blew over. I'd had to change my direction and outlook so many times over the last few months, and this was simply the newest plan in the never-ending line of new plans: First, Anonymous Tip. Then, Private Meeting. Pivot to Media Blitz, followed by Testimony. And now, Hibernate.

But what was I supposed to actually *do* during this time? I went from having so many things to figure out each day to having nothing on my calendar. No more legal calls. No more drafting letters. No more back-and-forth with senators. I couldn't work on writing research papers because I could barely make myself breakfast without feeling exhausted. I definitely couldn't go into my office; I could barely go outside. "Gray Blanket it is," I thought as I shuffled back to bed.

I also felt my anxiety rise with the gradual reduction of our security detail. I hadn't realized how dependent I'd become on their protection. There had been no question that we needed security in the lead-up to the testimony, when the media was calling me, Russell, our coworkers, and our friends and driving by our house and when strangers were making threats both vaguely generic and creepily specific. But that was also the time when we didn't go anywhere, so all the security had to do was keep us safe in our hotel room.

After the testimony, we were supposed to move forward with our lives and not have bodyguards following us everywhere. We couldn't afford it anyway—a full team with twenty-four-hour protection could run upward of $10,000 a day. I had the Go-FundMe money, which was a godsend for keeping us safe and adding security features to our house. I also ended up donating a lot of the money to college counseling centers, rape crisis hot-lines, domestic violence shelters, and mental health counselors at the YMCA and Boys and Girls Clubs. I needed to pay Deb back for the tens of thousands of dollars she'd put on her credit card in DC. Like it or not, I needed to scale back on security spending going forward.

I consoled myself with the reports about how much our risk had dropped after the vote. But there was still a lot of scary comments on the internet and vicious discussions on the dark web. A lot of information about me was being spread. I was still getting reports of all the threats from our remote team, summarized in eerie efficiency.

I couldn't go anywhere, even to a best friend's birthday party, without awkwardly asking for a list of everyone who might be there so they could be vetted by security. It wasn't worth it. I couldn't go watch my sons' soccer or basketball games. Neighbors reported that suspicious cars continued to park by my house, on a quiet street with no reason for cross traffic, at all hours of the night.

When Brett had gotten the job, I had focused on the fact that perhaps now the people on his side would back off a little. I suppose I underestimated this and completely ignored the fact that the people vehemently *against* his confirmation would double down on their opposition. Hundreds of protestors had descended on the Capitol with raised fists and signs reading "KAVA NOPE." Many of them were arrested. I heard that some protestors had even camped outside his house. I still knew many people who lived in his neighborhood or whose parents lived in his neighborhood. I thought about his daughters having to come home from school through a gauntlet of people talking about his high school and college antics. Then I thought about the threats I was getting toward my sons, particularly my older son. Apparently, there was still a tradition of targeting the firstborn, and many of the threats I received told me that karma was coming for my son. I found it so strange that both sets of kids, mine and Brett's, were having to experience such hatred pointed at their parents. But hopefully the people in front of Brett's house weren't threatening his daughters.

I had gone into the Supreme Court nomination and confirmation process thinking I'd need to get through a twenty-four-hour news cycle. I'd had no idea there would be four more years, multiple moves, countless news cycles, and plenty of front-page Supreme Court headlines to ride out before I attained anything resembling normalcy.

TWO THINGS CAN be true at once. You can be a privileged person with a lot to be grateful for. And it can still suck that your life is so limited, simply because you were honest about something that had happened to you. You can be ruthlessly targeted, and you can have more support than you know what to do with. You can hold space for both of those things.

You pay a price for telling the truth. "Gray Blanket it is."

One of the only times I left my hibernation in the first few months was thanks to the philanthropic businesswoman Laurene Powell Jobs. A week before Halloween, she invited my family and me over to her house in Palo Alto. I figured that if anyone had good security, it would be her. So we went, and she turned out to be one of the nicest people I'd ever met. She was also beautiful, with a radiant glow that was disarming. I was nervous and could barely eat the appetizer that was passed around before dinner, but by the time we sat down, I had settled in enough to try the soup—a gorgeous, rich bisque the color of the sunset. It was pumpkin or squash—I don't even remember; I just know it was the best soup I'd ever had. I asked for seconds, and we chatted about her work projects and the time she went surfing at Kelly Slater's wave pool. I loved picturing this goddess-like woman in the wave pool and sat rapt as she described what the wave was like and how challenging it was. She was just as interested in me. She asked if I meditated. She looked me in the eye and asked me how I was doing, how I was *really doing*, with complete and utter compassion and care.

She had invited another prominent Palo Alto executive and philanthropist. He'd also graciously helped us with one of our hotels at some point. He and Laurene were talking about what kinds of projects they wanted to do next, when he said, "Well, I've got Lars's thing next week."

My ears perked up.

I heard him mention something about a "fundraiser concert" and couldn't help myself.

"Metallica?" I asked. "That's my favorite band."

Everyone looked at me, not even attempting to conceal their surprise.

"Well, do you want to go?" he asked. "I'll get you good seats."

"When?" I replied.

"Next Saturday."

I looked at Russell, who raised his eyebrows as if to say, "If you're actually willing to leave hibernation, of course we're going."

I got home that night with more resolve than I'd had since the vote. I had to get over this and get it together. It was the motivation I needed. I felt like I'd gotten a little oxygen for the first time in months.

I told my security team that we would be going out in San Francisco next Saturday night, and they almost cheered. They were so happy to hear that I was getting out from under the gray blanket, to have fun, at night! Everyone was almost giddy.

Russell and I had never really used babysitters when the boys were little, which made it even more exciting to have the bodyguards there while we were gone. Talk about the best babysitters—the boys couldn't have been safer. I nearly skipped out the door.

But I felt unexpectedly emotional when I arrived. I hadn't been anywhere besides Laurene's house and therapy in weeks. It was similar to what we'd all feel a few years later when emerging from quarantine, where everything felt overstimulating and being around that many people at once felt threatening and thrilling all at the same time.

There was a charity auction before the show, and I bid on a surfing session with Kirk, the lead guitarist. I put in a starting bid for $10,000.

"We don't have $10,000!" Russell exclaimed.

"We won't win!" I assured him.

I wanted to get a T-shirt from the merch stand but felt too nervous to stand in line with people who might recognize me. I had been on every news outlet and in every newspaper just a month earlier, after all.

Before the concert started, someone from Metallica's team approached us and told us they could escort us backstage to meet the band. I nearly peed my pants. I'd never been so terrified. Well, maybe I had, in recent months. But this was anxiety inducing in a way that no flight or testimony could ever be. Walking into the room of senators, I had known what I wanted to say. This time as we headed backstage, I had absolutely no clue.

Of course, the guys were as approachable as could be, asking to take a photo (with *me?*) and laughing when I told them I'd bid on a surfing session with Kirk.

"We can go anytime," Kirk said, as I nearly melted into a puddle on the floor.

They put on a fantastic show, and I found myself actually dancing, singing, feeling euphoric. I texted Tory, wishing she was here with me, wishing we could go back in time to the way we used to be. "Omg," I wrote. "I told them about when we saw them at the Forum."

It felt good to leave my hibernation. I had no idea that I'd left my cave too soon.

Memo

I got home from the Metallica concert around two in the morning, absolutely buzzing. The band had invited us to the after-party, but it didn't even start until something like 4:00 a.m., which was like inviting me to a party on Mars. I realized that a friendship with Metallica might be a little more difficult than I'd thought.

I went to check my phone, which I'd blissfully ignored the entire evening, with the brief exception of texting Tory. We were heading into midterm election week, and there was usually a media dump during that time to try to distract from the real issues at hand. As Steve Bannon once explained, "The Democrats don't matter. The real opposition is the media. And the way to deal with them is to flood the zone with shit." I assumed I'd missed some news while I was at the show. But as I scrolled through the headlines, I saw my name over and over again. Any residual high I'd had from Metallica slowly drained from my body, replaced by a horror that spread through me, making its presence known in my chest, the pit of my stomach, even my fingertips, while my brain tried its best to convince me that what I was seeing was not, could not be, real.

The memo sent by Senator Chuck Grassley on November 2, 2018, was 414 pages. The subject line read: "Senate Judiciary Committee Investigation of Numerous Allegations against Justice Brett Kavanaugh during the Senate Confirmation Proceedings."

On page 3, it stated, "Committee investigators found no witness who could provide any verifiable evidence to support any of the allegations brought against Justice Kavanaugh. In other words, following the separate and extensive investigations by both the Committee and the FBI, there was no evidence to substantiate any of the claims of sexual assault made against Justice Kavanaugh."

That was pretty conclusive. "Why are there four hundred-something more pages?" I thought.

I read on: "Committee investigators later obtained a signed statement from Dr. Ford's ex-boyfriend, [redacted], casting doubt on Dr. Ford's credibility." "Brian," I mumbled to myself. The memo said he'd told the committee that I'd never mentioned my assault to him (probably true, though proving nothing), that I didn't have a fear of flying, and that I'd helped Tory prepare for a polygraph test.

Then this: "A classmate of Dr. Ford's at the University of North Carolina also provided a statement of doubt on her phobia of small spaces." I thought about a guy I'd gone to college with, Will, who had posted disparaging remarks about me on social media during the week of the FBI investigation. His profile page had Make America Great Again and Breitbart propaganda all over it.

The memo went on to Leland: "On September 22, Leland Keyser, a close friend of Dr. Ford, submitted a statement saying that she did not know Justice Kavanaugh and had no memory of the alleged gathering." Later in the report, it stated that Leland "felt pressure from Dr. Ford's allies to revisit her initial statement to the Committee that she did not know Justice Kavanaugh or have any knowledge of the alleged incident."

My eyes started blinking in rapid fire as I read about men I'd never met who lived in different states who alleged that they'd had encounters with me around the time in question that fit my description of what had happened with Kavanaugh but stated that each instance had been consensual. One of the men said that judging by photographs of Kavanaugh from that time, he thought they shared a similar appearance.

Another classmate from my undergrad days claimed that I had regularly purchased drugs and attended fraternity parties, alluding to an active and robust social life (which didn't disqualify me from being a sexual assault survivor—in fact, in many ways, it had been my coping mechanism). Another statement refuted my descriptions of how the attack had affected me, pointing to my extracurricular activities during college and saying that I didn't seem to be afraid to be confined in places with one exit.

Just when I thought things couldn't get any more unbelievable, another person with name redacted said that she had seen a close family friend's photograph of me with George Soros, taken several years ago, suggesting that I was part of some liberal political agenda. There was a note that the woman had agreed to forward the photo to the committee but failed to do so and that it had since been proved to be false. I would later mull over the fact that 4,500 tips had been called into the

FBI and had gone uninvestigated, while this phony photo was still included in the government memo as relevant information. Claim after claim was presented, including that I'd been unfaithful to Brian while living in Hawaii and that I'd committed credit card fraud.

Names were mostly redacted, but I felt confident I knew who most people were. Brian was easy to identify, as his name and accusations had already come out in the week of the investigation. And Will had made his stance pretty clear during this time, though others from this period in my life could have made claims about me. Louis, a friend from high school who had been in my brother's class, had made himself known early on after the *Washington Post* story. He had posted some extremist political content on Facebook but had also sent me a message saying that he wished we could be back on the beach, playing together as young kids. Then suddenly, he was posting comments saying that I was lying, that he was going to reach out to his contacts in the FBI and tell them, "We all know who she really was." He said that I had sex in my car with all the boys from school (despite the fact that I went to an all-girls school and didn't have a car or even a driver's license until the spring of my junior year).

At first, I felt betrayed by people I'd considered friends, even people I'd loved. But the more I learned, the more I realized that they were just cogs in the machine of a much larger mission to find people from my past and discredit me. It appeared that the opposition forces were systematic about it, finding one from my high school days (Louis), one from my college days (Will), and one from grad school days (Brian). I could be angry with these people from my past for saying what they said, but when it came down to it, if they hadn't stepped forward, then the opposition would have found other people to do the same thing.

It was one thing to be ripped apart on social media and random message boards and another to have lies legitimized in a government document. I wanted to do something but was flung right back into the confusing maze of decisions I'd wandered when trying to figure out how to bring my allegations to light pre-nomination. How do you refute a memo published by a US senator that calls you a drug dealer, a credit card thief, and a pathological liar?

Should I write an article? Go on TV? You can't sue the Senate Judiciary Committee, can you?

My team told me to just stay quiet, saying that anything I did would only draw more attention to the memo. They assured me that it was not something the general public would read. My friends seemed to feel the same way. I lamented to them, "It's in the congressional record that I've bought drugs! Our government is making stuff up about me! They are taking the word of terrible people!" Everyone told me not to worry. One person told me that the memo was about as significant as a tree falling in the forest. I felt like I'd been lit on fire and everyone was just walking by.

I was desperate to right the wrongs, even the ridiculous ones. I asked my PR people, "Can we just put out a statement that in those days women never had to pay for drugs?" In my memories, drugs were practically thrown at me. I never saw money exchanged.

"God, Christine," they said. "We're not saying any of that."

I talked to Senator Kamala Harris and asked if they could at least take it off the Senate Judiciary's homepage. She was supportive and sympathetic but said that since the Democratic Party didn't have the majority, that was not in their power. She assured me that the Democratic senators would respond and that one way or another, I would have the last word. Dianne Feinstein responded to the Grassley memo in an interview, saying that we shouldn't treat survivors like this.

In a final attempt, I went through the memo and annotated it, sending my refutations to anyone I thought might be able to help. They expressed their sincere apologies.

I went back into hibernation.

A few days later, a historic midterm election ushered in a "blue wave" of progressive wins, including a record number of women elected to Congress and significant successes for LGBT candidates as well as religious and ethnic minorities. Alexandria Ocasio-Cortez became the youngest-ever female member of the House at the age of twenty-nine. Democrats were ecstatic. I received numerous messages saying, "This is in no small part because of you." I glanced down at my gray blanket. Was this what victory looked like?

I was still hung up on the memo, and would be for a long time. It was all I could talk about. If I'd written a book at that time, most of it would have been a tirade against that damn memo.

The thing was, while people tried to console me and downplay the impact, I knew that it would have a domino effect. Even if most people never read the memo, it would be used for more articles, books, and public takedowns arguing that I was a mess, a terrible person who couldn't be trusted.

I saw it referred to as Brett's "exoneration." If he was being vindicated, what was happening to me?

No Good Things

I thought that as a result of the Grassley memo I'd been banished from society, but there were still many people who wanted to talk to me. My PR person presented me with what felt like a million things every day: interview requests from cable news channels, morning shows, *The Ellen DeGeneres Show*. The producers of *Ellen* offered to send a car to drive me from Palo Alto down to LA to be on the show, but when I imagined it, I could only picture a crowd laughing as Ellen danced around and I just cried onstage. I said no to everything.

One day they informed me that *Sports Illustrated* wanted me to present the Inspiration of the Year Award to a fellow sexual assault survivor, Rachael Denhollander, at their Sportsperson of the Year Awards.

"Who is that?" I asked.

"The first gymnast to come forward about Larry Nassar," they said, referring to the USA Gymnastics team doctor who had sexually assaulted hundreds of gymnasts during his career.

I googled Denhollander and saw something she'd written in support of me. "That's nice," I thought, but I intended to graciously decline since I was still planning to hibernate indefinitely.

Then I started watching videos of her speaking. The first thing that struck me was how totally okay she seemed. In one of her talks, she spoke about jumping off the metaphorical cliff before knowing if anybody else would but feeling certain that she needed to do it even if she was the only one. I hadn't heard my own feelings expressed so eloquently before. "I have to paddle out for this girl," I thought. "How could I not do this?"

"Well, you're turning everyone else down," my PR person said when I agreed to do it. "You really don't have to."

"No, I really have to do this," I said. "As long as I can record it and not have to be there in person. Just prop me up in a chair and give me a teleprompter. Almost no one will see it anyway; it's just for the people at the awards ceremony. She's the big deal, not the person presenting her award."

They agreed to let me film my speech, and for reasons I wasn't quite sure of but also didn't want to argue against, I was invited to meet the Golden State Warriors basketball team at their practice. It was an uneventful Monday evening in downtown Oakland, save for the fact that I found myself in the same gymnasium as the players who had won three out of the last four NBA championships, a team that many were saying had revolutionized the way the sport was played. I brought my friend Tanya and my basketball-obsessed sons, feeling like this was a tiny redemption for how much I thought I'd failed them over the last few months. They watched in awe as their heroes performed drills and took shots, witnessing perhaps the best group of players who had ever been collected on one team. I didn't expect any of the coaches or players to talk to us, but

Steve Kerr came over to thank me for my courage. One of the assistant coaches came up and introduced himself, telling me that my testimony was the best example of citizenship he'd ever seen. I was honored, and surprised that one of the most validating descriptions I'd received about what I'd done was delivered to me on a basketball court. Then Steph Curry came over and literally took the shirt off his back and the bracelet off his arm and gave them to my kids. Pictures from that day show the boys looking like vagabonds, dressed in the same four pieces of clothing they'd been wearing on repeat after living out of a suitcase for so long. They were so happy, almost delirious. It felt really good to give them that moment, and it buoyed them from the realities of our circumstances.

The next day, a camera crew descended on our temporary house to film the award presentation. My friend Tanya came over and did my makeup. I was wearing a Volkswagen shirt, which my team vetoed, so I put on one of the outfits I teach in. The producer told me the whole thing would probably only take an hour.

I guess hindsight is 20/20, but I realize now that having a camera in my face while I read a prepared statement and a bunch of strangers stared at me was too much like reliving the terror of my testimony. They hadn't brought a teleprompter, and we soon discovered I was in no state to memorize anything. My brain couldn't keep more than a few words together, so they had to feed me the speech line by line. There was an endless loop of stop, retake, stop, retake. I remember saying the phrase "I'm in awe of you" so many times it started to sound like a foreign language. Hour after hour passed, and everyone became increasingly exasperated.

The awards ceremony took place a couple of days later. It was telecast on NBCSN and posted on YouTube. My team told me that under no circumstances should I read the online comments. Of course, I opened them up immediately. Just as I'd scrolled through the Grassley memo, reading statement after statement about what a terrible person I was, the comments on the *Sports Illustrated* award speech brought punch after punch, with hardly a positive remark in between to let me catch my breath. There were hundreds and hundreds of them.

I was forced to face the fact that it wasn't just Chuck Grassley, some conservative extremists, and a handful of people from my past who hated me or wished me harm. A lot of seemingly regular people who had no connection to me whatsoever also hated me. The ratio of negative-to-positive comments convinced me that a massive section of the population considered me a liar who should be in jail—or worse. I thought of all the letters and phone calls I'd received from people saying they wanted to kill me. Maybe there were even more of them than I'd thought.

I felt terrible that I had brought any kind of negative response to Rachael's award. I asked my team to help me send her an apology for ruining what should have been a major achievement for her.

"No, she's happy!" they responded. "Wait, are you reading the online comments, Christine?"

"Of course I'm reading the comments," I answered. "I feel like I have no idea what's going on these days. I'm trying to figure out everything I can."

They assured me that the comments were skewed, reminding me that the people who followed and commented on *Sports*

Illustrated content were not representative of the general public, that this was after all a magazine that featured photos of women in their bathing suits. They said the overall response had been overwhelmingly positive.

I thought back to a few weeks earlier, when I had researched the *Sports Illustrated* Awards and seen that Colin Kaepernick had won the Muhammad Ali Legacy Award the previous year. I'd admired that they had selected someone so polarizing, someone whom people either loved or hated. Now I was that person, and I realized it was the hardest way to live, because the intensity on both sides felt misguided. People loved me for the wrong reasons and hated me for the wrong reasons. In that case, do you have to either accept them both or dismiss them both? I couldn't come to terms with either option.

My team was urging me to "just focus on the positive," and I tried. At least my kids got to meet the Warriors. Honestly, even I had had fun at the practice. Which was perhaps the problem. Maybe there was a connection between having a good time and paying the price. The correlation began to form in my mind, confirming that I should probably do nothing rather than risk more retaliation.

I went back into isolation, with the exception of a meeting with legal advisers in an upscale San Francisco hotel lobby, where I also met David Hogg, the Parkland school shooting survivor turned gun safety activist who became one of the founders of the March for Our Lives. I felt immediately at ease with him, as if he were a friend of my sons, and when he asked me how I was doing, I answered more honestly than I had the hundreds of other times I'd been asked that since my testimony.

"Probably a lot worse than people think," I admitted, trying not to vent about how bad it was but feeling safe with him and too exhausted to sugarcoat things.

David totally got it. He had been mocked, harassed, and threatened. He'd been the target of conspiracy theories falsely accusing him and his classmates of fabricating the shooting. Congress members had hounded him, TV hosts had made vulgar and violent comments about him, and he had faced multiple murder attempts. He was only eighteen years old. I felt a maternal-like pride as he told me, "We stand with you and the #MeToo movement," before leaving for the airport with only a small backpack.

After that meeting, I ordered some of the books written by the Parkland survivors for my sons, who got really into the work they were doing. My older son started a March for Our Lives chapter at his school, and my younger son took a bittersweet comfort in learning about what the survivors had gone through. As the youngest in the family and the one who had been kept the most in the dark about what was happening, he had the hardest time living away from home for so long. These kids gave him some perspective on his own situation. One day he told me, "Those kids were *actually shot*, which is much different than people wanting us to die." I didn't know whether to be proud of him or angry with our country for what these kids had on their plates. I guess I was both.

As with Rachael Denhollander, meeting David Hogg showed me what I could learn about survival from people much younger than me. I was struck by his courage and amazed at how he'd redirected his trauma into purpose and resolve. The misinformation and smear campaigns that had led me into isolation had motivated him into action. When I told him that during our initial meeting, he waved it off, saying that living in a gated community helped. It was more than that, I assured him, and we fell into an easy rhythm, riffing on the strange world we'd found ourselves in.

David was the first person I'd met who seemed to truly understand what I was going through. I mentioned the dilemma of balancing this two-sided coin of admiration and hate, and he nodded in recognition.

Someone snapped a photo of us on my phone, and when I looked at it, I saw that both of our smiles looked forced, despite the warmth between us.

"If you smile for the cameras, you get more hell," David said. "People saying you're doing this for profit, stuff like that."

I nodded, thinking back to what I'd heard after my testimony: that I could never be anything other than who I was on that day.

We joked that there was no fun allowed for people like us.

But even though we said it jokingly, there was truth in that. I'd had the time of my life at the Metallica concert, only to come home to the Grassley memo. I'd been an excited fan at the Warriors practice, only to get knocked down by the online backlash to the *Sports Illustrated* award. Perhaps I needed to accept the reality: I shouldn't do anything fun ever again.

Exclusive

Bears are known for hibernating, but they're not the only animals who do it. Certain species of squirrels, hedgehogs, chipmunks, bats, frogs, and snakes hunker down for the winter to conserve energy. For these animals, hibernation is a survival mechanism. But it can also leave them vulnerable.

If there's one lesson that I learned in the aftermath of my testimony, it was that the Machine would stop at nothing to rehabilitate Kavanaugh. They'd viciously attacked not only me but also those around me. Determined not to let what had happened to Tory happen to anyone else, I disconnected from most of my friends, spending the few hours that I socialized each day with my lawyers and PR people.

Lawyers and PR people can be remarkably effective at solving certain kinds of problems. They are not, however, the place to go when one needs a hug. And, as much as I tried to fill the void created by withdrawing from my friends with strategy sessions focused on combating the ever-increasing stream of disinformation being unleashed against me by right-wing media, it wasn't working. I craved warmth but was stuck in hibernation mode.

Enter two journalists (including the one my lawyer had introduced me to the morning after my testimony) who were prominent in the coverage of the #MeToo movement. Here was the empathy I hadn't been able to order off a room service menu. Here was the casual rapport I missed from the beach and the pool. Refreshingly nice and disarmingly friendly, these two women weren't arguing one side or spinning messages. They were truth-seekers, like my psychologist friends, offering a compassionate ear that was informed by the years they'd spent speaking out on behalf of women. But they also just felt like real people. I'd been told to remember that "the media can be very friendly, but they are not your friends." But in my mind, anyone trying to help me was a friend.

And honestly? They were lovely. They traveled to visit me. They made it clear that they were on my side. One day, one of the reporters told me she could help me go see my younger son's basketball game. I'd been missing all of my sons' activities, not wanting to put them at risk or cause any sort of distraction. It killed me, though—I had never missed a game in the past. It was kind of my favorite thing to do.

"I'll go with you and block you," the reporter offered.

We went to the basketball game, with me trailing behind her in a baseball hat. In her tailored, all-black newsroom attire, she almost looked like my bodyguard. We were there for an entire minute before people started noticing me. The coach came running up and hugged me. A couple of parents came to say, "We're glad you're okay." (*Was* I?) Others smiled from afar. We didn't stay long, but it meant a lot to me that the reporter had tried to help.

After we left the game, she and I went with my friend Jean

to a strip mall right next to the court, where we could get some wine and all-you-can-eat ribs. The reporter had a child who was younger than mine and Jean's, and we joked that we were giving her a preview of what her life would look like in a few years.

"It's hard in the beginning, but it gets better."

She was just like one of the gang. Little by little, she pulled me back out of my cave.

NOT LONG AFTER, I was invited to a private dinner at Gwyneth Paltrow's house. The reporters had arranged it, describing it as a special event where some of the Weinstein and Trump assault survivors would be gathered to talk about their experiences of coming forward. I voiced my uncertainty about being included, and my lawyers told me that we could also "work on stuff" with the reporters while I was in LA. That's what ultimately got me. I couldn't resist the temptation to try to fix all that had gone wrong.

As fate would have it, shortly after I agreed to go, I found out that there was a memorial concert for Chris Cornell, the lead singer of one of my favorite bands, Soundgarden, happening in Los Angeles the same night as the dinner. A bunch of musicians, including Metallica, would be covering his songs. Had I been in Palo Alto I'd have regretfully missed it. But now I would be in LA! I couldn't not go. I got tickets and just figured that I could hurry to the concert after dinner.

IF YOU'D LIKE to know what Gwyneth Paltrow's house is like, the main thing I can remember is that there was a lot of white and that, for a movie star's mansion, it was remarkably under-stated and cozy. The main thing I remember about Gwyneth herself is that she could not have been nicer. Her hospitality was sincere, and I found myself wondering why she seemed to be someone people either loved or loved to hate. "These people on the internet don't even know her!" I huffed to myself as I saw her welcoming the guests and making sure everyone was comfortable.

Inside the house, I found an entire room full of people who'd come together to participate in a book the reporters were writing, a sort of sweeping narrative of that period of reckoning during 2017 and 2018, when notoriously abusive but previ-ously protected men had come toppling down from their po-sitions of power. The energy was genuine and palpable. And they'd gone out of their way to welcome me and make me feel included. But they were celebrating, and I was barely surviving. I felt awkward, out of place, and, ironically, alone.

I found myself next to a gorgeous woman who I recognized as the actress and activist Ashley Judd. Not knowing what one says to Ashley Judd at a #MeToo meetup, I told her I had a cold and was not drinking.

"Well, I don't drink," she said matter-of-factly. "Let's have some tea."

So there I was, in the corner of Gwyneth Paltrow's living room, drinking tea with Ashley Judd as she told me about the new relationship she was in. It was such a relief to lose myself in the details of her giddy excitement for a few minutes. I asked if I could sit next to her at dinner.

"Would you please?" Ashley replied.

Soon we were seated for dinner at a long table. I seemed

to be the only person aware that there were mics on all of us, or at least the only one who cared. As the others conversed, I stayed silent. At one point, I said something about my parents, regretting it as soon as the words left my mouth. I imagined the sound bite broadcast on the news that night.

"What am I doing?" I thought. "Chris Cornell's memorial concert is happening right now a few miles away, and I'm not there. I don't belong here and they don't need me. How do I leave?"

But I was trapped. I was on the side of the table against the wall, seated toward the middle. There was no way to casually slip out. I confessed my predicament to Ashley, who couldn't have been cooler about it as she encouraged me to go.

"You deserve to have fun," she said, and I tried to believe it even as the thought of "no good things" hovered in the periphery of my thoughts.

Leaving in the middle of this dinner would be potentially the rudest thing I'd ever done. It went against my upbringing and everything I'd been taught. But my love for Soundgarden went even deeper. I couldn't wait for a break in the conversation. I couldn't wait for the next course. Finally, I just got up and whispered in Gwyneth's ear.

"I'm really sorry, but I need to leave," I said. "I had plans to go to this concert."

"Who's playing?" she asked, clearly surprised but more amused than offended.

"It's a thing for Chris Cornell."

"Oh yes, I heard about that!"

She stood up and said, "I have an announcement. Dr. Ford is leaving to go see Metallica perform at the Chris Cornell tribute."

Everyone looked confused. Gwyneth smiled. I fled.

We'd already missed a good chunk of the concert but got there in time to see Metallica perform a perfect four-song set including "For Whom the Bell Tolls," and Miley Cyrus nailed her tribute, passionately singing "Say Hello to Heaven." The remaining members of Soundgarden closed the show—without Chris, of course—a lone microphone symbolically standing center stage. After they took the stage, people started filing out, grumbling that the show was getting too loud. I couldn't believe it. They didn't get it. The painfulness of it all was the point. I sat with my friend Mika and the other megafans we'd befriended as we watched and cried together.

The next day, I got in touch with my PR people, apologizing for leaving the dinner early.

"Why did you even go?" they asked.

"I thought I was supposed to?"

"You didn't need to be there."

"But you told me to meet with the reporters."

"Yeah, meet with them for like thirty minutes, answer a few questions," they replied. "Don't open your door to them and spend every day talking."

Translation: Don't go to reporters for a hug.

Right, I'll add that to the handbook.

IN RETROSPECT, I shouldn't have spoken to anyone besides Russell and the kids at that time. I understood logically that the journalists who swept in after a major event were probably not destined to become real friends. But they were the closest thing I had access to at the time. They were so generous with their time, expressing real empathy for the turmoil and reverence for my testimony—all during a period I needed it the most.

I wasn't *completely* oblivious—I knew they were writing a book about the #MeToo reckoning that had happened. I mean, clearly; otherwise, why would they be hanging out with me? But I had tried not to dwell on it. It made me slightly uncomfortable and self-conscious to be compared to all the brave activists on the front lines of the movement, and the dinner at Gwyneth's house had magnified those feelings. One of the reporters, noticing how quiet I was that evening, pulled me aside, saying, "I hope you don't feel like there's too much attention on the other women." I was confused, as that was the furthest thing from my mind.

I was really worried when I got back to Palo Alto. I talked to my lawyers about it, asking, "Why don't they just write a separate book, then, or just not have me in this other one?" Their book had been almost finished by the time they met me, and including me just seemed like an unnecessary addendum. Listening to my PR people's suggestion that I pull back on the relationship, I asked that my chapter be the same size as everyone else's and said that otherwise I didn't want to be included at all.

The dynamic between us shifted after that. They seemed resentful, saying I was withholding, not allowing them to do the work that would help so many women. I felt pulled between the reporters asking for more and my PR people telling me not to talk so much.

Meanwhile, the reporters kept asking me to hand over a letter I'd written to Jeff Flake, saying their editor needed to see it. They called me as I was sitting in a salon chair at a hair appointment, with aluminum foil crowning my head.

"I'm here with my editor," one of the reporters said curtly. "Cough it up."

"This isn't what you said it was going to be like," I said. "You sound so different right now."

That was the last time I talked to the reporters. They'd told me back when we were on a daily-chat basis that by the time I read the book, each line would be predictable—that's how closely they would follow what I told them. When the book came out, I noticed that most of what we had talked about was nowhere to be seen.

Now, let me be clear: I know I wasn't always easy to work with, and I felt foolish not understanding how journalism works. But I felt a little betrayed. Nevertheless, I have to acknowledge that the reporters were just doing their jobs. They are not the bad guys in this story.

The truth is, sometimes it's easier for me to shift blame to the people closer to me than it is for me to pinpoint how evil the higher branches of organizations like the Federalist Society can be, or how the people in Congress can get away with a blatant disregard for justice—and individual lives. It's easier for me to say, "People on my team didn't tell me this, and that was kind of fucked up," than it is for me to say, "I was destroyed by a huge amorphous machine that has its fingers in every branch of our government and is beyond anything I can control."

Whatever explanation there is for why things soured with the two reporters, I should have learned my lesson. But I didn't. And I wouldn't. The same pattern kept playing out over and over again—another journalist would come along, someone who was "on my side," who would *finally* get things right. Each arrival of a new project brought hope that the errors of the prior could be undone. I would share with them as much as possible about what happened. They would interview my friends. I would hand over text message threads to ensure that nothing got lost in the shuffle. I'd spend hours upon hours walking them through my story.

Then their book would come out, and I'd read it and feel my world turning upside down all over again. "That's not how it happened," I would speak back to the pages. "I must have been unclear," I'd tell myself. "Next time, I'll have to be super precise. Maybe I need to write out every single thing that happened, day to day." The next journalist would show up, I'd tell them what had happened in the past, and they'd assure me that they would make sure to get it right this time. Then I'd see what they ended up publishing and admonish myself for being so dumb.

Another reporter interviewed me in early 2019 for a book she was writing, pitched as a broader look at the Supreme Court. Even though it was written without bias and she portrayed me fairly, the process still brought to light some troubling realities. And the conflicting recommendations I was getting about who to talk to or not talk to was head spinning. Were people looking out for my best interests, or trying to get exclusives? There was a lot going on behind the scenes that I had no way of knowing about. I saw everyone as an informant, even Brett himself, who I'd heard had traded information across the political aisle. I'd even heard that he was so pissed about the Supreme Court book he'd called the author late at night to complain about the way he'd been portrayed.

It would later be confirmed that Brett had been a confidential informant to the journalist Bob Woodward. The legendary journalist had wanted to expose Brett during the confirmation hearings as an anonymous source for a book he'd written years earlier but had been talked out of by his editor, and the piece was never published. They could have spoken up right after I had, adding to the information on the table. But they didn't. I would read about it, annoyed that evidence of Brett's disclosures had been kept under wraps while I took the fall as a lone whistleblower. "Where's that story?" I wondered.

HERE'S AN UNCOMFORTABLE truth: even if the reporting was Pulitzer Prize–worthy, I'd probably never be happy with the end product of *any* attempt to tell the story of what happened. The content is traumatizing and makes me feel terrible. I can admit that I am a little biased and might not be the best judge when it comes to the merit of these projects. But it's the process itself that turns it from something difficult to something that messes with my reality. If it were a simple transaction and something got lost in translation, I could live with it. But there's this false sense of closeness, promises made to fix everything, time spent cozying up to my friends and helping with my security issues, that makes an inaccurate or distorted story feel like a personal betrayal. When someone tells you that they are going to paint you as a hero and then when all is said and done you feel worse than before, it feels like the opposite of the justice you so desperately seek.

After more times than it should have taken for me to finally call it quits, I decided I wouldn't talk to anyone from the media anymore. The psychological warfare it put me through was just too exhausting. I was used to academic writing, where everything is based on evidence and inference from data. I thought journalism was the same. But it's not. I know now that journalism—at least the kind I've been exposed to in a personal way—is about telling stories. I understand now that some of these people knew the story they wanted to tell before they even spoke to me. And it's not their duty to help me.

I have to help myself.

That's a large part of the reason I'm dredging all of this up again, hard as it has been. It's up to me to get my story down the right way. But I've been conditioned to mistrust, to communicate as if I were walking through a field full of verbal land mines. I have to remind myself constantly that *I* am the one writing *this* book and that my words will not be restated in a different way or printed without my approval. I still can't seem to wrap my head around the fact that this time I'm in control.

No more pretend friends, I've decided.

But then there are the people who never pretended to be friends in the first place.

River of Deceit

As a surfer, you get asked a lot of questions about sharks.

Personally, I love sharks and believe in the Native American lore that seeing one is a good omen. Sure, some are apex predators, but not all, and most of the ones off the Santa Cruz coastline are juvenile white sharks who are more likely to back away from a large surfboard, ceding to what they perceive as the larger, more powerful creature. In a study conducted by researchers at California State University Long Beach Shark Lab, it was found that juvenile white sharks came close to swimmers, paddleboarders, and surfers multiple times every day over the course of the two-year study, and the sharks never attacked once. Sharks are more opportunistic. If they come upon the carcass of a seal or a whale, they'll scavenge it.

In 2019, I was essentially a carcass in the water. And the scavengers came to feast.

Political operatives had pounced on whatever information they could find about me early on, as evidenced by my LinkedIn page views and all the downloads of my research papers. Obviously, there wasn't much for them to work with. But when the

Grassley memo came out, they went to town. I was told there would be negative books written about me, essentially taking the Grassley memo's information and putting it into longer chapters. "Smear books," they were called, most written by people with ties to the Federalist Society or the America Rising PAC or the conservative strategists who had worked behind the scenes during Brett's nomination and confirmation.

I lived in fear of these books and what they would say. Most of them were announced on the heels of a nonpartisan book titled *The Education of Brett Kavanaugh*, written by two journalists who aimed to provide a balanced account of the confirmation process. The smear books were decidedly not balanced.

I thought back to the philosophical conversations I'd had on the beach, when Kirsten and I listed every bad thing we'd ever done. Would these books put all those embarrassing details into print? Would they go even further, concocting lies that gained legitimacy through the authority of being published?

Again my team told me not to worry, that these were fringe books that no one would read beyond their own extremist audience. Months later, the books were published, and some of them hit the bestseller list. Apparently, people *were* reading these books. Apparently, I would go down in history as a drug dealer and a liar.

It felt like when I was told that my testimony would be televised and I assumed it would air on C-SPAN. Then seemingly everyone in the world had seen my testimony. By that same logic, everyone must have read these smear books or seen what the right-wing websites had written about me. I was embarrassed to even take the trash out in front of our temporary house, assuming every person on the street who saw me considered me a diabolical liar on a mission to assassinate the character of an innocent man.

Grunge had always been my comfort music, gentle and mopey, and it felt particularly appropriate to listen to during this time. There was a Seattle band from the mid-90s called Mad Season, formed as a side project with members from other bands, including Pearl Jam and Alice in Chains. Their first single, "River of Deceit," was an immediate hit, and while it was written about the singer's drug addiction, its lyrics spoke to me as I read lie after lie about my past, my personality, and my purpose in coming forward. I listened to the singer Layne Staley gently cry, "A head full of lies is the weight, tied to my waist / The river of deceit pulls down."

I was weighed down by the words in these smear books, pulling me in one direction, down, down, down. I wanted to shout, "I'm already dead! No need to keep dragging me!"

I thought about sharks, opportunistic scavengers. They'd pick me apart until there was nothing left.

WITHOUT A DOUBT, the worst thing I've ever been through was this period of the smear campaigns.

There's a term, DARVO, introduced by psychologist Jennifer Freyd, that stands for "deny, attack, and reverse victim and offender." It refers to a manipulation tactic used by a perpetrator (say, a sexual offender) who is called out or held accountable for their actions. In response, the accused reverses the roles to blame the victim, while also taking the role of victim on themselves. It's gaslighting to the maximum degree, and it felt like half the country decided to team up and DARVO me in 2019.

I was getting doxed left and right, as people found my personal information and sent it out widely with the suggestion that "something" be done. Fake accounts were created in my name. Some of them were taken down; others could not be removed and continued to spread misinformation. If there had been a handful of imposters, I might have done more, but just as there'd been in the lead-up to the testimony, there were so many. What could I do? I might have gone after a few people. But I couldn't go up against an army of them.

People were logging on to the City of Palo Alto's website and pulling up plans of my house to show that Russell and I had not been doing a home remodel at the time we went to couples therapy, trying to find some hole in my timeline that could refute what I'd said. They tried to prove that I was lying about putting in a second front door in our home, that it was not an addition attributable to my PTSD and safety concerns but actually an office through which I ran a private practice.

Others were saying that because I'd worked on research that involved the use of abortion pills (not to abort fetuses but to treat Cushing syndrome, a deadly disease of the hormonal system), I had come forward as part of a conspiracy to keep an antiabortion judge off the Supreme Court. It was true that I'd analyzed data for the company. But now people were photoshopping pictures of me with the pills.

None of the people on Brett's side seemed to be afraid to speak up for him. They cherry-picked facts and footage to show what an upstanding citizen he was. But it felt like no one on "my side" at the time wanted to fully align themselves with me. I couldn't believe more people weren't speaking up for me as I was being dragged through the mud, accused of being a drug dealer, a prostitute, a child molester. With the exception of Speaker of the House Nancy Pelosi, Senator Kamala Harris, Senator Mazie Hirono, Representative Anna Eshoo, Representative Jackie Speier, and a few others who checked on me and offered tangible help in the year that followed the testimony, most of the people from Congress did nothing. Granted, I wasn't asking them to. But weren't they supposed to be public servants?

Nancy Pelosi took a meeting with me in May 2019, as I prepared for the smear books to come out. I went back to the amateur investigation I'd put together in the aftermath of the Grassley memo, giving her a list of untrue or malicious things that had been said and done and my refutations of each. I was impressed with the complete and undivided attention she gave me, even as her office buzzed with visiting foreign ambassadors, constituents in waiting rooms, and staff members bouncing around. Her competence could not have been higher. She didn't promise to fix everything, but she said she'd look into it. It gave me a little hope.

Toward the end of our meeting she told me, "I think you need to turn to the arts." It was unexpected, as I was in practical defense mode, trying to expose liars and right wrongs. Instead, she was suggesting that I portray my story in a way that could do it justice. The same way that the movie *Erin Brockovich* had brought mainstream attention to the issue of groundwater pollution, perhaps there was a general audience for my story and a more artful way of telling it. It planted a seed.

In the meantime though, I was still swimming in regret. I should have followed up with Anna Eshoo fifty times before the nomination. I'd tried to do what I could before Brett was selected, but I hadn't realized that without me just completely throwing myself into the process, crucial time would slip by. I was talking to Larry about it one day, telling him I should have just come out on July 3 and said, "Hey, everyone, this is the deal." Larry stopped me and said, "No, Christine. If you'd come forward at that time, you would have never made it to testifying. They would have just destroyed you before you were able to have the impact you ultimately did.

"Let me walk you through this," he continued. "Here's how it would have gone down. You would have gone public on July 3, before the nomination. Opposition researchers would have gone to work and discredited you within a week or two. By July 15, no one would have spoken your name again. Staying anonymous for as long as you did was what allowed you the chance to tell the truth."

It was ugly but true, gruesome but comforting. I had to stop underestimating the evil that these people were capable of. And the reality that they would never give up.

That's what scares me about this book. Why would I open myself up again? Why would I throw myself back out to the sharks?

But unfortunately, whether I speak out or stay quiet, I will always need to worry about them. And no matter what I write in this book, they will do their best to tear it apart. They're scavengers.

The Gift of Fear

We moved back home on Christmas Day. Not because I wanted to—I would have preferred to stay under my gray blanket at the temporary house watching the Surfing Channel all day. But our boys needed to return to a sense of normalcy. Russell had already moved back in with the dog, ready to turn the page on this chapter. I looked around at the white walls and saw that they'd been stained with my sons' handprints. It was time to go.

Going home meant I'd need to let go of the in-person security guards who had stayed on part-time, since they would draw more attention to our home and perhaps make my neighbors uncomfortable. I'd never been good about keeping the bodyguards undercover. I was always introducing them to whomever I was with, asking them if they wanted anything to drink when they were supposed to be invisible. They were probably relieved that I wouldn't be stepping on the backs of their shoes anymore, but I didn't want to lose the peace of mind they brought me. I'd gotten used to knowing that my sons were in good hands. They had driven the boys to and from school and their various activities, and as a mom of kids who played sports, I had enjoyed handing over my chauffeur duties for a little while.

Walking into my house that Christmas morning, I had the sudden urge to get rid of everything. To make my home feel more like a hotel. Some sort of coping mechanism, I suppose. Russell and I opened up the garage door and started putting everything on the street for people to take. Stereo equipment. An aquarium. Decor from previous places we'd lived in and never unpacked. I got rid of almost all of my clothes, having realized over the past few months that apparently I only needed about eight items of clothing.

I was so happy. A little fake Christmas tree that came pre-strung with lights sat in the corner. We had no gifts to exchange besides some pajamas and Patagonia jackets and the presents my parents had sent for our kids. The excess of presents in the past had always made me uncomfortable. This was the way I thought Christmas should be—a small tree, not too many presents. The boys were so stoked to be home.

I took the gray blanket and spread it across my and Russell's bed.

By spring, I'd received multiple messages about the situation at my Palo Alto University mailing address. Other faculty members were missing letters and checks because the mail room was so full of letters and packages addressed to me. It was finally time to pick up my mail.

I brought Keith with me, and thankfully I also brought my truck, because there were tens of thousands of letters. We loaded one box after another into the bed of the truck. My friend Jean recruited some people from our community to help open the letters, and soon middle school girls were volunteering to simply help cut open the envelopes (reading the actual letters would have been a step too far), and women my own age and older were pulling out particularly compelling messages. We weren't sure what we would do with them but thought about creating a website where people could share their stories. I wanted to rent a tour bus to visit some of the survivors who had reached out and asked to speak with me. I eventually had to get a group of doctoral students who were experts in trauma psychology to help me with the herculean task, taking a hundred or so letters at a time, opening, reading, labeling, and sorting. Most were supportive and moving beyond words. Others were not.

There was one pile labeled "HATE." It was smaller than the others, but it almost vibrated with rage. I stared at it like it was a dog about to attack me. Some of the letters were prophetic, warning me of the devastation this would have on my life (as if I wasn't aware):

May you live with your lie to eat at you forever. Many woman [sic] I know have no compassion about your person because of you [sic] accusations without fact or evidence.

Karma was a recurring theme:

You lied for the sake of selling your soul to the Democratic Party. . . . you're a fake a liar and a disgrace to every women [sic] that has been abused . . . you played stupid and you acted stupid . . . you're nothing but a piece of shit and a loser . . . God has a special place for people like you and it's called Hell. . . . Don't ever forget the word karma because it has your name all over it . . . it will get you it always does.

You liberals seem to take such pleasure in destroying your political opponents, but karma is real, and things seem to eventually come full circle.

They were mostly typed out, sometimes handwritten, and occasionally illustrated (violently). It intensified the horror of it all to consider that they'd taken the time to find my address, pay for postage, and have it delivered to my doorstep. While the positive letters usually came in colorful Hallmark envelopes, I began to watch out for the ones in white business envelopes addressed in thick, Sharpie-scrawled block letters, with a PO box as the return address.

There were times I didn't realize it was a hate letter until I'd read a few sentences. They would start out very professionally, talking about "going through the evidence," and then by the next paragraph they'd be calling me a bitch. Some were absurd in their intensity:

A "Dr" of Psychology who needs a therapist? Has to go to couple counseling? One who cannot solve her own problems? A JOKE!!! . . . I have been raped and I have no need to seek counseling. . . . You don't think YOUR 2 sons are going to do EXACTLY what you state Brett did to you? Seriously? You have ruined their lives with YOUR BIG mouth and inability to be an ADULT. . . . $10 says your husband leaves you. . . . If I ever see you in public—I will spit in your face.

You are a fucking ugly psycho bitch! Who in the hell would want to fuck you anyway? You are no looker! Very plain and ordinary. Nothing special! . . . (too bad Bill Cosby didn't get you)

Others were more straightforward threats:

We know where you live, we know where you work, we know where you eat, we know where you shop. Your life is over. [Picture of the grim reaper included.]

But even those threatening ones weren't the "you have to leave your house" letters. I started handing over the scarier mail to security and law enforcement, who said they would follow up on any letters that had come from somewhere within an hour of my house. The long-distance death threats they didn't really make a fuss over. They looked for proximity (if someone could simply drive to my house and do something about their fury, they were more dangerous) and future-tense threats (as in psychology, if you told a therapist you *had* killed someone, they would have to maintain confidentiality, but if you said you were *going* to kill someone, they would be legally obligated to take action).

I began to see patterns, similar statements being used. It felt disturbingly organized, as if there were a coordinated effort to send me messages about George Soros or pictures of me being strangled. The hate mail also seemed to increase right before an election, as well as around New Year's. I pictured people sitting at home with a glass of champagne, making resolutions for the new year, and writing me a letter to tell me I'm terrible.

Each time I read a piece of hate mail, I'd put it down and think, "That's a real person out there." It was a strange feeling to be so close to violence but not in its grip. It's kind of like getting in a fender bender—your cortisol is rolling, you're feeling shaken, but you're not in immediate danger.

I would sit and repeat the most troubling messages, trying to attach a human face to each one:

> You ruined that man's life. But we're good, you've got sons. If karma doesn't hit you, it will definitely be hitting them. Good thing there's two of them, so we have two opportunities to retaliate.

THERE'S A DIFFERENCE between being scared and being terrified. Being scared can be almost invigorating. When I see a shark breach in front of me, I'm automatically filled with adrenaline, but it's not negative. It's more of a state of hyperfocus, with chemicals surging through my brain, shutting down what's unnecessary and sending all my energy toward what will help me survive.

Being terrified feels like the opposite. It stops me in my tracks. Instead of fight or flight, it's freeze. I never had to feel terrified when we had physical security details because they were on top of everything. But opening up these letters and reading "We want you dead," "I give you a year," "We haven't forgotten about you," "We're coming for your firstborn"—that's fucking terrifying.

When strangers come up to me, most just want to thank me or take a selfie, but others look at me with a flat expression and say, "I know who you are." It sends shivers down my spine. People have tampered with my car. I have a call blocker on my phone, but I still sometimes receive creepy phone calls and voice mails. I was grabbing a drink with a friend not long ago, and a guy came and sat in our booth, saying, "You girls look like you're having fun." He went on to tell us that he was from Washington, DC (my pulse quickened), that he went to my brother's school (my internal alarm went off), that he worked in Homeland Security (I wanted to run but I was literally blocked in by him). There was even one incident when a real estate client of one of my friends who had submitted an affidavit corroborating my story looked back and forth between her and a large kitchen knife, saying ominously, "I've been reading about you."

On the day in October 2022 when Nancy Pelosi's husband Paul was violently attacked with a hammer in their San Francisco home, I had a meeting with my security coordinator, who recommended added caution and security since such extreme things were happening. Oddly enough, I'd just found a dead animal in my yard. Perhaps it was a fluke. Perhaps it wasn't.

I wrote a message to one of Pelosi's colleagues to be passed along to her, expressing my sadness over what she and her family were going through and thanking her for her service and patriotism. She wrote back immediately. I couldn't believe it, but then I thought about what a multitasker she'd been in her office. I guess I could believe it.

"Please give my warmest thanks to Christine," she said. "My heart breaks for her."

AT SOME POINT, someone gave me a book called *The Gift of Fear* by Gavin de Becker, a security expert who helps government agencies, corporations, and public figures predict and prevent violence. "That's the last thing I need," I thought. "I already have the gift of fear a thousand times over. No need to fan the flames."

But despite myself, I cracked it open and found it fascinating. It went against much of what I'd been taught in psychology. When you're learning about anxiety disorders, the focus is on distancing yourself from your fearful thoughts since anxiety by definition is about overestimating the probability of a bad event. This book suggests the opposite and tells readers to not only listen to their fears but to overestimate the worst-case scenario. In my professional life and in my own personal experience with anxiety and PTSD, I had been told to take a breath and understand that the danger in my mind was not actually happening. *The Gift of Fear* told me to tune in to what *might happen*. De Becker argued not only that your more alarming thoughts could be real but that focusing on them could be useful.

Everyone from my lawyers to Russell and my friends had been trying to ease my worries, and then Gavin de Becker gave it to me straight: If someone's compelled to kill you, they will kill you. So there's no point in worrying about that. However, there may be others who want you dead but will only make it happen if there aren't enough obstacles and consequences.

He laid out a practical guide to address the latter set of

people, which essentially entailed layering barriers so that there's more resistance to their mission. One core strategy is to create various hurdles around your home that act as little checkpoints someone has to pass. First they have to cross a fence. Then a light might go off. Then a dog barks. With each layer, they have to pause, allowing ambivalence to work its magic. Each time, they become more likely to give up.

It felt weirdly calming to get access to the thought process a potential attacker goes through. It felt like there was a scientific method behind it, and that made it less foreign—and therefore less terrifying—to me. The person might wave in front of a camera to see if there's a motion sensor alarm. If not, they know that next time they come back they don't have to worry about that. "Makes sense," I thought.

The book hammered home time and time again that security is peace of mind. "Don't I know it." I nodded. De Becker explained that it only takes one person to harm you out of the thousands who are simply threatening to do it. Whatever it takes for that peace of mind is worth it. So I painted the house a different color. Moved the address sign. We installed yet another door in the breezeway (an added layer) and made it bulletproof, along with our windows. I thought back to how we'd lived in the house before all this. We would always have our front door open, the boys zipping in and out. Now it was a fortress.

I hired an intelligence agency to assess my house and install cameras. They were smart and tactical. But I would need to bring on more security measures in the years that followed, and that necessary peace of mind came at a cost. An annual inspection, twenty-four-hour camera sweeps, and ongoing consultations during specific incidents can run upward of $150,000. Even the GoFundMe donations could be used up quickly at that rate. There were also bills from lawyers and PR people, just for deflecting threats and keeping my name *out* of the news. I had never imagined how expensive it would be to just chase normalcy after testifying.

"Few acknowledge that healing is costly," Chanel Miller writes in *Know My Name*. "That we should be allocating more funds for victims, for therapy, extra security, potential moving costs, getting back on their feet, buying something as simple as court clothes."

As I budgeted out what we could afford, I thought how impossible this would be for so many other survivors. If you don't have the resources, how do you even leave an unsafe situation? If I, with all my privileges, could barely afford to speak out, what did that mean for so many other women?

SECURITY COSTS ARE still a concern these days, but I probably don't need to tune in to my fear anymore. I think I'm good.

I've landed somewhere in the middle on the spectrum of psychology training and *The Gift of Fear*. I've adapted to a state of low-grade vigilance, but I don't think I live in constant fright.

A thought turns itself into an emotion, which is then acted out. So my fear shows itself more in my behavioral patterns now. If I were qualified to diagnose myself—which I'm not— I'd say I am classically avoidant, a trait that is closely connected to anxiety disorder and PTSD.

I used to love going to new places, but now I exclusively go to about four places in my everyday life. I've become such a creature of habit. But I've also learned from the experts that if someone is casing you, being predictable and going to the same places makes it easier to figure out your patterns. So I try to take random trips and disrupt my normal habits. But I also don't like being in the car anymore, especially as a passenger. I get a little panicked. I used to love taking road trips and would regularly drive from Palo Alto to Los Angeles every weekend to surf. But now it's a big deal for me to go to a new coffee shop. Another thing I've learned from the experts: If you think someone's following you in your car, don't drive erratically to try to get them off your tail. Just get into the right lane and drive super slowly so they are forced to blow their cover.

Most days, however, I'm not walking around thinking somebody is going to take me out. It's more like the feeling you get when you're alone at night in your house and you're getting ready to go to bed. You lock the door, close the windows. You don't think someone's outside waiting to break in, but you also don't want to take any chances.

Research shows that people with phobias collect other phobias over time. I'm aware that I'm vulnerable to spiraling. But yesterday the house alarm went off, and I was simply annoyed by the inconvenience.

One last bit of advice from the experts: get a dog. When we first got ours, her constant barking was problematic. We were researching trainers to help "fix" her. But then all of this happened, and I was told she is one of our most valuable security assets. Good girl.

The Kindness of Strangers

I haven't eaten at my dining room table in years. It is covered in stacks and boxes of letters from survivors and supporters, once neatly organized and now a bit frenetically thrown together and less classifiable than they once were. They spill over onto a cabinet along the wall, boxes above and below. Artwork is in one corner. A blanket made by women at a shelter in Oakland hangs on my living room wall. Behind our piano is a large box of the longer narratives, not just people writing to say "This happened to me too" but those telling the entire story of their assault. I want to collect those to be used for research or perhaps send each one back to their representative districts as constituent data so their elected politicians can see the scale of sexual assault. The others, I plan to donate to some sort of library archive or a museum that might create an exhibit out of this overwhelming collection of hope and comfort.

I should probably put everything in storage in the meantime. I'm sure Russell would like our dining room back. My sons' friends must think I have a hoarding problem. (My sons have gone blind to the piles by this point.) But something keeps me from clearing them out. Because in the midst of the Grassley memo, the smear books, the death threats, and the online harassment, there were these voices scribbled and typed and sent to tell me to hang in there. I look at the letters and hear the lyrics to the song "Help Is on the Way" from the seventies rock group Little River Band: "Are you always in confusion? Surrounded by illusion? Sort it out, you'll make out."

The voices in these letters were the flip side to all the people who were hell-bent on taking me down. Instead, many of these letter writers told me I was nothing less than a hero, the definition of bravery. Neither side was 100 percent right; both were too narrow in their view. But while the side that hated me almost sent me into permanent hibernation, this other side wrapped me in a hug and eventually gave me the strength to believe in the goodness of people.

The letters themselves were astounding. Some of them were a bit devastating. The students who were helping me would catalog each letter, and I could tell whenever they came across a particularly heartbreaking one. Since I hadn't picked up the big batch of mail until half a year had passed since my testimony, I was able to handle them a little better than my idealistic students were.

"Ah, you got one of those letters," I'd tell them as they wiped tears away or struggled to collect themselves. "Go ahead and stop for today."

Just as I'd done with the hateful letters, with each message of encouragement, commiseration, or validation, I would remind myself that some stranger out there had taken the time to convey their feelings and get them to me. I would try to picture the face of each person behind each letter.

Then there were the faces and names that I already knew but that belonged to strangers offering a dose of kindness all the same. In the lead-up to my testimony, actresses including Kerry Washington and Debra Messing posted messages of support—Washington proclaiming "women must be heard" and Messing holding a sign that read "I believe Dr. Ford." Jane Fonda tweeted "We stand in solidarity with Dr. Christine Blasey Ford." Tarana Burke was in the room when I testified and would write later about breaking into tears in the bathroom during a break. Gloria Steinem contacted me and graciously invited me to several events, even offering to host me at her apartment.

And then there was Oprah.

She wrote me a letter maybe a week after I testified. My PR team told me she had been so moved, she left a meeting to go sit under a tree and detail her admiration and understanding, as a survivor herself. She mentioned in the letter that she would love to talk with me further.

"Do you want to get on the phone with her?" my team asked.

"Absolutely not," I responded. Even in my regular life before all this mess, I might not have been able to talk to her. But in my current state? No way.

It's silly to imagine now. Who wouldn't leap at the chance to talk to Oprah? (Honestly, I wish she would call me right now.) But that was just not the case at that moment. Speaking with Oprah then seemed more like a potentially embarrassing opportunity than an honor, because I could barely function at the time.

"You kind of have to respond to Oprah, Christine," my PR people said.

They helped me write a response, telling her that I wasn't doing very well, that I needed some more restorative time. Oprah wrote back that she totally got it and would be ready when I was in a space to talk.

There was still a bit of pressure from my team—after all, you don't want to let an offer from Oprah expire—so we arranged a phone call for the following week. The conversation is a blur in my mind, but I remember saying that I couldn't believe she lived near Rincon, one of the greatest surf breaks in the world. I told her that I often went down there in the winter to surf, and she said to let her know the next time I planned to visit.

I took her up on her offer in the spring of 2019, when I drove down to Pepperdine to accept a Distinguished Alumna Award. On my drive home, I planned to surf Rincon and then have coffee at Oprah's, an itinerary that felt about as ridiculous as saying I was going to play pickleball with Jennifer Lopez.

But just as with Metallica, I needn't have worried. Oprah was warm and welcoming, and I enjoyed the best coffee of my life. The conversation flowed despite me being more than a little in awe of her and our surroundings. She was a professional interviewer, after all. She asked me lots of questions with genuine interest: Did I like to cook? Did I garden? I mumbled some noncommittal answers, not wanting to admit that I didn't really do anything other than think about the events of the last year. I noticed that when she brought up the testimony and its aftermath, she talked about it exclusively in the past tense, as if it were all over and done with. But for me, it was still very much happening in the present.

The conversation turned to surfing, which allowed me to relax further and even educate her on her neighborhood surf break and some surfing lingo. At one point, I mentioned the saying "Never drive away from good surf," which refers to the classic mistake of thinking the waves might be bigger at another break. You might find superior waves, but the spot will be more crowded. Or you will have wasted the best time of the day in your car.

"I like that," she said. "Never drive away from good surf." I could see her absorbing the message behind it.

When it was time to get going, she walked me out to my truck, handing me a stack of books to read as I thanked her over and over. I needed to bungee cord my surfboard down more securely for the rest of the trip, and I waited for her to head back to her house. But when she saw the bungee cords in my hand, she grabbed one and walked to the other side of the truck so we could connect them. She was wearing a perfect, crisp white blouse. My Toyota Tacoma was covered in dust and dirt. I couldn't hide the look on my face.

"What, do you think I don't know how to do this?" she asked, nonchalantly hooking one end to the side of the truck bed and holding the other out to me so I could connect it to mine. I stretched my bungee cord over the board, nearly shaking because I was so nervous that she would soil her white shirt on my dirty truck. She wasn't worried at all.

When we got the board strapped down, I looked at her and said, "I can't believe you did that."

"Next time you come through and need help with your boards, let me know," she laughed.

AFTER THE PEPPERDINE award, all the smear books came out, and I lay low on awards and appearances for a while, not wanting to be a liability to whatever organization was brave enough to recognize me. But that also meant that the only things I was hearing said publicly about me were bad. When the ACLU of Southern California decided to give me the Rodger Baldwin Courage Award in November 2019, my PR people told me to go, figuring it might be good to hear people say nice things about me for a change. Judd Apatow would present me with the award (which I had no idea would turn into an ongoing friendship—he became a great ally and source of support).

I decided to drive down for the ceremony so I could surf Rincon, which also meant hitting up my pal Oprah. When I told her my plans, she suggested I stay at her house the night before so I could be well rested for the ceremony. "No fun allowed," my brain warned me as I contemplated the invitation. "No good things." But I had enough sense to know that when Oprah invites you to stay at her house, you don't say no.

I accepted and immediately realized I had nothing to wear. I didn't even have a proper set of matching pajamas for this slumber party at Oprah's. Would she give me a pair, like it was an episode of her Favorite Things? I didn't even have a normal suitcase. Would I really walk into Oprah's house holding the duffel bag I took on surf trips? I told Russell my predicament, expecting him to wave me off and tell me not to worry, but he immediately went to Macy's and bought me a new suitcase.

A few weeks later as I walked into Oprah's home for the second time, I felt slightly scared but also safe. Her security was seamless, so good it was unnoticeable 99 percent of the time. For at least this evening and the following morning, I would be taken care of.

"Nice suitcase!" She smiled as she greeted me.

The next thing I knew, Oprah was driving me around the property in a golf cart. She seemed so *normal*, hopping into the driver's seat, slamming on the accelerator. She exuded such laid-back serenity it was impossible for me not to relax.

We had dinner that night in Oprah's dining room over-looking the Channel Islands. I had more of that unreal coffee the next morning at breakfast, chatting with Stedman and Oprah's godson Will, who brought his adorable new puppy. As we said goodbye, I felt restored in a way I hadn't since leaving DC.

Oprah is obviously an almost unreal example of generosity, but the ways in which she cared for me were simple. She offered solidarity as a survivor. Coffee as a friend. A safe space in more ways than one. Oprah was pivotal, at a time when I needed it the most.

So were the letter writers. Words simply don't do justice to what their compassion and tenderness did for me. The kind-ness of strangers has been the thing that's been hardest to quantify in all this.

As I've written this book, I've often worried that it will come off too negative, that in describing the horrible aspects of what happened to me, it won't properly pay tribute to the people whose care literally kept me alive. The debt I feel toward them is what has pushed me to tell my own story despite the personal risks and the return to the spotlight that I dread. I have to write them back, in one way or another. They saved my life.

That's not hyperbole. There were so many times throughout the last five years when strangers felt like family. And unfortunately, there were also times when my family felt . . . strange.

Thicker than Water

Dr. Glenn Patrick Doyle, a popular psychologist who specializes in PTSD, has written about trauma survivors being sensitive to good-natured teasing, something I've struggled with most of my life. I grew up with constant playful taunting, which I desperately wanted to be cool about but which pushed a button that made it impossible. The tears would come, then I'd feel silly for being so sensitive. The next time it happened, I would try to roll with it—which required me to deny who I really am. Instead of acknowledging that I felt judged or criticized, I would become who I thought I needed to be. Little by little, my identity would start to slip away.

At my wedding, one of my brothers gave a toast that centered on how much money I'd cost my dad, referring to me as the most expensive child in history. He rattled off all of my costly adventures, from grad school in Malibu to the internship in Hawaii and now a wedding at the Ritz-Carlton. He even brought out a piece of paper, saying he was representing my dad as a lawyer and needed Russell to sign an agreement stating that my dad was no longer financially responsible for me. Everyone else was cracking up, but I thought it was a little harsh. However, I was also so happy in the moment, with Maw and Russell sitting next to me, that I just went with it. I didn't want to find myself in the role I'd tried to escape: the Problem.

I've SPENT YEARS reconciling my role in my family. I'd often felt like the odd one out, too emotional. I knew that a certain amount of stiffness was generational, that feelings weren't really in the vocabulary of many people from my parents' generation, but I also saw families around me that noticed when someone was melancholy, who stopped and asked, "What's wrong? How's everything going?" I craved being seen in that way.

Whenever something bad happened, my family avoided talking about it. If anyone did bring it up, even casually, everyone would get upset at the person who addressed the issue. The next day, it would be over and done with. My family didn't understand my uncomfortable sentiments. If I was upset, it was because I was sensitive, unable to take a joke.

And perhaps I was. As much as I can say that my family was harsh at times, I also have to admit that I wasn't the easiest person to live with as a kid and a teenager. I gave them a lot of trouble. I was a bit selfish—I have to cop to that. And even when I put thousands of miles between us, I was still the one who made waves.

My mom and dad had always been actively supportive, traveling annually to visit me and my family and hosting us every summer. They never forgot our birthdays and always traveled to every graduation ceremony (mine and my kids'). They did the best they could, and once I was an adult and a parent of teenagers myself, I understood them a lot more. Unfortunately, some past dynamics showed up with my dad in the aftermath of the testimony and swept me back in time. What my dad didn't do—defend me wholeheartedly in his media statement—was not hard to process. What he did do after I testified was problematic.

In the fall of 2019, one of my advisers asked me about a letter from my dad to Brett's dad. A book by a *Washington Post* reporter was planning to include mention of it, and they were giving me a chance to respond.

"Oh, no," I replied. "I'll ask my dad, but I'm sure he wouldn't have done that."

When I checked with him, he gruffly denied ever writing a letter.

"Are you sure you never wrote him a letter, Dad?" I asked again.

"Why do you keep asking?" he said. "I already told you, I never wrote him a letter. And I already gave a statement to the media."

My team told me that a reporter had proof, that it would be included in their book whether I approved or not. They asked me if my dad would want to make another statement. I was confused. They had advised me to not draw any attention to the last book that was written. Why did we need to address this one? To feed a media cycle? I assured them that if I asked my dad a question directly, he would never lie about it. There was nothing more that needed to be said.

I stuck by my dad and vehemently denied the possibility of any letter.

Still, I called him a second time. "They're saying they have a copy of an email you wrote."

"Oh." He paused. "Well, I did send an email," he said.

"What?" I replied, trying to make sense of this sudden reversal.

"You said 'letter.' I never wrote a letter. But yes, I sent him an email a few days after the vote." The letter versus email reminded me of the talk with the Feinstein staff—"it must be a letter not an email," "you can just email the letter."

I closed my eyes. "No. No, no, no."

"It wasn't a big deal," he said. "It said something about, 'I'm glad Brett got confirmed so we can all put this behind us now.' Just gentleman to gentleman." A classic "my dad" move. Manners are everything.

I felt like a fool. I had been insisting to everyone that there was no way my dad had reached out to Brett's dad. I was uncharacteristically silent and wanted to get off the phone. He was also uncharacteristically silent. Finally, he said, "I should have just said, 'I'm glad this is over.' That's what I meant."

"Got it," I said.

Sitting at my desk at the Stanford Center for Advanced Study of Behavioral Sciences, in the office once occupied by George Schulz, I started to bawl, shutting the sliding glass doors so other Fellows wouldn't hear. It didn't think it was possible to drop down further into the abyss. I called Russell and he drove up the hill, consoling me while we overlooked the Hoover Institution and Stanford campus, our beloved alma mater. Russell rationally talked to my lawyer on the phone about his disappointment in the lack of protection I'd had in this quandary and questioned why people would focus on my father. "I feel for the guy," I heard Russell say, and the noisy response his comment induced. After hours of rehashing the topic and all things "I can't believe," it was getting dark outside.

"It's just a book," Russell said to me after the call, and I half laughed. He was the perfect combination of laid-back and fiery, declaring it both unimportant and ridiculous—all the books, the email-letter, and the suggestion that my dad make a statement. I went with it. I had testified fourteen months ago. We settled on walking to our car and not missing a chance to spot the beautiful owls, turkeys, and coyotes, the hillside locals that ventured into the parking lot after dark.

As it all sank in, I held tight to the recent weekend in Rehoboth Beach that I'd spent with my parents. Only a couple weeks earlier, I had spent a few perfect days with them, just the three of us. They had spoiled me with crabcake dinners and drinks on the porch and watched me take a swim in the Atlantic waters where I grew up, afterwards wrapping me in a towel like I was a little kid. I was determined not to let this fiasco undo such a restorative weekend together.

Now I tried to understand my dad's intentions. He wanted to do what he felt was the proper, polite thing, extend the olive branch. I thought about all the times I'd congratulated a colleague on a promotion even if it hadn't been deserved. I knew that my dad's country club was like an extended family to him. And his relief about the confirmation process being "over" wasn't unfounded—I'd clung to a similar hope, that I would get less backlash if Brett was confirmed. But the part that hurt was how soon he'd sent the email, extending a proverbial congratulations to the father of my attacker.

I didn't talk to my team or my dad for a little while after

that. I needed space to process—alone. It had been both a public slap in the face and a simple confirmation that my dad was my dad and the media was the media (perhaps I should have listened to my dad on that front). I embraced radical acceptance. It was gutting, until it became clarifying. "Of course," I thought.

Simply put, my dad's response was not the one I would've ordered off the menu during this ordeal. But I'm probably not what he would've ordered either.

IN THE PAST year, I've come to a sense of peace about my parents. It's nuanced. I can't talk about feeling like they didn't help me without pointing out the reality that I had left decades earlier, moving across the country and minimizing trips to DC, always opting for the summer home in Rehoboth. I can't talk about moving to Los Angeles and breaking free from the DC prison without acknowledging that my dad was the one who unlocked the door and made it possible for me to escape. I can't describe the way he hurt my feelings without pointing out how much he has helped me to get where I am and that he now takes incredibly loving care of my mom. I can't talk about the public actions he took before, during, and after the testimony without recognizing that he also sent me loving texts of support and forwarded so many supportive letters from his friends.

We don't talk about what happened. (As for my brothers, other than a brief hello at family events, I've only heard from one of them, once, in the years since the testimony.) It's not totally okay, but it's okay enough. My parents live far away, and we're all getting older.

Anyway, what's the alternative?

The letter writers' experiences give me wisdom and comfort. For every batch that reads, "I wouldn't be alive if it weren't for my family" or "only my parents stood by me," there's another batch that reads, "even my own family believed him."

Certain things can make me sad. Watching surf contests and seeing the winner dedicate everything to their parents can bring me to tears. Most of all, I miss long visits to see my parents and East Coast family, and the option to talk to my parents about anything and everything. My dad was always the one who was happy to go through any decision and impart an opinion even if it wasn't exactly delivered with a spoonful of sugar. I still ask his advice on parenting and career stuff, but some things I no longer fully share with my parents or anyone. When I do talk to my dad, he is always fully immersed, asking questions, giving his expertise. He and my mom are and have always been A+ grandparents. But some things in life you have to do alone.

Working through this alone, I've reached my greatest sense of empowerment in an unlikely place: the abyss. Where even if no one on earth were to believe you, you know it still happened. No one can take that away from you.

Boys and Girls

It feels fitting that I had two sons. I was always a guys' girl, hanging out with surfer dudes, chummy with my male research colleagues, friendly with the mostly male fans at Metallica and Guns N' Roses concerts. I'm laid back; I can talk sports.

But I am most definitely not a cool mom. When my eighteen-year-old son wanted to go to a three-day hip-hop festival, I allowed him to go only if I was there too. I annoy my high schooler at the pool when he's working a lifeguard shift. I get overly involved in picking my kids' classes. I'm very engaged and present.

I have friends with daughters the same age as my sons, and I see the way their parents fear sending them out into the world on their own.

I am scared for my sons too, but in a different way. My kids have a target on their back because of me. But that's a unique situation, unlike the almost universal fear that parents of young girls possess. They have to live with this worry constantly under their skin about the danger inherent in being a young woman. I can't imagine what that's like.

I was fifteen when I was attacked at a high school gathering. My older son was fifteen when I told him what had happened to me and when he watched me testify. My younger son is now seventeen, the same age Brett was on that fateful night. I think about a teenage Brett, and then I think about my teenage sons, and the dichotomy between them is overwhelming. I think about my older son responding to my confession of assault with, "I'm sorry that happened to you." I think about my younger son getting hurt by a girl at school and pretending it didn't bother him. I can't imagine them ever making a girl feel unsafe.

I can't say I parent differently because of my own sexual assault. Of course I want my sons to be respectful and responsible if alcohol is around. I want them to understand and abide by consent. I also know that they can be clueless and make me cringe and that they still have more to learn about gender equality. But I've watched them wrestle with toxic masculinity and the hefty expectations we place on boys. I've heard them talk to their friends about unfair power dynamics. I've met young men like David Hogg who show me that if we can listen to the boys who aren't afraid to break out of the boxes we've put them in, if we let them lead, we may not have to fear as much for our daughters. What I've seen in my boys gives me hope for the men (and women) of the future.

I WOULD NOT have guessed that young women would provide my main inspiration as I navigate my own journey as a survivor and a reluctant whistleblower, but they've really shown me the way forward. I've met people like Aly Raisman, one of the gymnasts who testified against Larry Nassar in the monumental sexual assault case, who called me terrified the night before her testimony and then took the stand and demanded justice. I've met with Chanel Miller, the Stanford sexual assault survivor who shed her anonymity to speak out about the flaws in our legal system and support for victims of sexual assault. We hung out at her grandmother's house, which is a stone's throw from my own. For a meeting between two sexual assault survivors who had been plucked from obscurity and thrown into unnerving public roles, our time together was joyful and refreshing. We laughed over candy and tea, to the point where her grandmother peered into the room to check in on us.

I remember being struck by the ages of the senators in the room when I gave my testimony to the Judiciary Committee. So many of them were so old. Then I think about the youngness of the people who have given me hope on this journey. I've seen boys rewriting the scripts that were given to them. I've seen girls take the trauma they've gone through and transform it into action. While I was working on my laptop at a café recently, a woman came up and left me a note saying that she had gotten a master's degree in gender studies because of me.

As a professor, I've always known that the teaching goes both ways. But I never thought that the teacher would also become the student in terms of healing from trauma. The takeaway from all of this that I never saw coming is that I can learn the most from people who are half my age. Younger generations are doing the work of meaning making in the face of injustice and outrage. They inspire me and give me hope that I thought I'd lost. They've given me the best road map for my own reentry into the world.

The Road to Recovery

For an entire year after testifying, I didn't teach. I mostly only left my house to go to therapy, or a friend would pick me up and we'd hike the Dish, a popular trail in the Stanford hills named for a huge radio antenna that looks like the world's largest satellite dish. We'd process whatever bizarre news had come out about me and sing silly songs at the top of our lungs.

Then the pandemic hit. I'd been essentially locked out of my house for months, and now I was locked in it. It was undeniably scary and tragic, but given my specific circumstances, it was also kind of awesome. There was no pressure to go anywhere. The news cycle was dominated by more urgent stories. I happily went back into hibernation for a while.

When things improved and going out became a necessary evil again, I realized I could hide in plain sight by wearing a mask. Then eventually enough time had passed that I could mostly go to large events and public spaces without fear of recognition because anybody can look familiar if you look long enough. I could see people staring at me, trying to place where they knew me from. I would try to avoid talking, because my voice usually gives me away.

I was finally able to return to teaching, where my students were tactful and respectful, and I went back to Santa Cruz for the summer, where people are more into the politics of marijuana and Airbnb restrictions than of the Supreme Court. Most of our neighbors never even brought up my testimony, except for a couple down the street who kindly told Russell once, "We're big fans of your wife."

My grief cycle started with the customary denial—my "someone's going to fix this" phase. Every so often, I would get little glimpses of hope. During Trump's impeachment, people asked me if I was encouraged by the possibilities, thinking that if they held Trump accountable for all of his wrongdoings, there might be some retroactive justice across the board. Or additional allegations would come out against Kavanaugh, and there would be speculation that he would be impeached. I would dabble in the bargaining stage of grief, negotiating with the universe for something amazing to happen that would somehow counteract everything I'd gone through.

But every time more information came to light about Kavanaugh or the way the confirmation was handled, various contacts in DC would tell me the harsh truth: there is zero chance that anything will be done. It was initially hard to hear, but I appreciated the transparency. I now know the difficulty of asking a bureaucratic organization to disrupt itself when everyone involved—even the people on my side—want to just keep the processes going as they are.

There are days when I feel pretty good and others when I log into Facebook and see one of those "10 years ago today" memories, with a photo of me and my sons floating on surfboards or outside the Giants stadium during the World Series or building a sandcastle on the beach. Sure, I can still go to the beach with my sons, and now I can take them to baseball and basketball games, but these days I'm always wondering if someone is going to take pictures of me or if some scary person is going to approach us. I mourn the loss of being so carefree. I take another spin around the grief cycle.

One of the hardest parts of trying to recover from all this is that I feel like I can't be myself anymore. I used to be a fun person, but I was a big downer the last few years. Everyone wants me to get back to the person I was, but I don't know if she even exists anymore. One day, my younger son asked me if I could please be happier. It broke my heart, so I ran around the block with him at 10:00 p.m. and shot basketballs at the hoop in front of our house.

Some people cope with trauma by never mentioning it again. Some cope by talking about it almost exclusively. In the last five years, I've been in the latter camp. Most conversations have wound their way back around to all this. But in the last few months, there have been times when I noticed that I'd gone the whole day without talking about it. Then a new threat, or a new documentary, or a new book came out, and the grief started all over again.

I get the sense—make that "I know for a fact"—that some people think I'm taking too long to get over it, much longer than they'd like. They ask me how I'm doing, but they only want the answer if it's "Great!" I tell them that I'm still getting death threats, and they respond, "Why would people still care?" They don't want to know the real answer. They don't want to hear the long story. They want me to move on.

I heard a saying recently about speaking from your scars, not from your wounds. I can see that in my near future, like a light at the end of the tunnel. I picture myself at a dinner party, telling a story about when I testified in front of Congress, like it's a fun fact.

In the meantime, I tell myself, "Don't let this take over your entire psyche." But if I suppress it, it will get even worse, right? So instead, I oscillate between both ways of thinking. I tell myself that I'm done, that I'll just move to a small town, teach at a community college, and listen to grunge music all day. But something still gnaws at me. It feels like I still need closure. So I decide to go all in, speak up for myself, and control the narrative. Then I get further into that game and realize I don't think I want to do that either.

For the first few years after testifying, I was in self-pity mode. It was not an intentional self-absorption (and my therapist tells me it's a normal part of the trauma process), but I was so incapable of seeing anything past my own problems that I couldn't even comprehend anyone else's grief. One of my close friends had a parent pass away in 2019, and I just completely missed it.

I've made progress over the last year or so. Now I can create space for other people. I can go with a friend to her chemo treatments. I can help a friend dealing with a divorce. I can show up for my friends the way they showed up for me, on the beach, at the pool, in the testimony, and in ways I never could have imagined.

The last few years have shown me that it's never the people you expect who'll take your kid to school and do all the pain-in-the-ass errands for you even though their kid goes to a completely different school. The people who take your very poorly behaved dog and let her live with them for months while you stay in various hotel rooms. The people who take you on hikes up in the hills so you can yell and scream and sing Metallica songs (very poorly). The friends who order french fries, let you hide under your blanket, and then pull the blanket off and say, "We're going on another hike." For as much as this story involves disappointment and dread, it's also a story about the power of really great friends who step in when you need them the most.

So many people stepped up for me, and then there was Russell, who has always stood beside me. Others have propped me up in desperate times, but he's in it for the long haul. He kept working through all the chaos to take care of our family. He took care of the dog when she fell on the list of priorities. He is a perfect foil to my indecisiveness, my apprehension. He and our sons have carried me through this with unconditional love.

WHEN I MET Anita Hill in 2019, I asked her, "How long after your testimony did you go back to teaching?" She responded, "However long I was in DC, about three days." My eyes went big, and I admitted it had been about a year since I'd taught a class.

"It was different back then," she reassured me. "And my students were an important source of support."

I didn't think she'd had it any easier than I did, but I fantasized about not having to deal with nasty comments and trolls on the internet. Because she was a lawyer, it seemed like Anita knew what was reasonable to expect. I had hope. It was my coping mechanism and my Achilles' heel. I asked her how long it would take for me to get over the whole thing.

"Twenty-five years does a lot," she said.

She was a lot younger than me when she testified. If it took me twenty-five years to recover, I'd be seventy-seven by the time I could move on.

"I don't think I can wait that long," I said.

"Well, give it five years," she said. "You'll notice a big difference."

I've passed the five-year mark, and I definitely see a change. I can be a real friend again. I can talk about other things. I'm not checking the date every day and comparing it to what was happening five years ago. I can do something other than repeat, "I can't believe . . ." Now I can believe.

There are even parts of this ordeal that I can look back on fondly. Spending so much time in hotel rooms and temporary houses with my sons is something I'm weirdly grateful for. We had never spent so much time together. I'd never had time to listen to them talk for hours about their favorite hip-hop groups or basketball players. It felt like we were in a strange little snow globe together, insulated from the world. I know that I've come a long way in my recovery because when I think about those room service cheeseburgers now, they actually sound pretty good.

The healing that's come with time, therapy, and a worldwide pandemic has allowed me to strip my life down to the essentials, showing me what I really do and don't need. This experience has completely rebooted my life. I no longer say things like "when things are normal again" or "when I'm better." The other day, I noticed that a box of hate mail had gone missing. I'm not sure if I should attach a symbolic meaning to that. But I'll take it.

Epilogue

Sometimes something extreme happens in your life, and it gives you a brief moment of clarity.

My life has rarely been clear. I'm not organized. I don't like making decisions. I arrive at work and figure out my lesson plan when I get there. And I've mostly gotten away with it. I'm too old to change now.

However, there was a fleeting moment of clarity in 2016, when my life seemed to be imploding: I was diagnosed with uterine cancer. I was overstaged, meaning that everyone thought it was much more serious when in fact it was in the very early, treatable stages. I only found this out after several months and multiple surgeries. But when I thought I was dying from cancer, everything became razor sharp in my mind: these are the toxic people in your life; these are the people you should appreciate more; this is what matters; this is what doesn't.

Two years later, my life *actually* imploded on a worldwide stage. The clarity to come from that experience has taken much longer. And by the time it arrived, it felt like the world had moved on. It was as if the world patted me on the head and said, "What you did was great, thanks, but there's something else we're all focused on now." I went from being on the cover of *Time* magazine to feeling like I'd been pulled offstage. A one-hit wonder. An answer on *Jeopardy*. "Oh yeah, that woman . . . what was her name?"

Because the rest of the world got consumed with more pressing matters—a pandemic, racial injustice, climate change, war—I felt like I was supposed to stay quiet. And in many ways, that would have been easier to do. Staying quiet serves my best interests and safety, without a doubt. But it also serves the people who *want* me to stay quiet. And I'm not ready to give them that satisfaction. I also owe it to myself to break the silence.

Reliving it all during the process of writing this book has brought out an intense physiological response. I've gotten overstimulated and been thrust into a state of fight or flight. (There's a new response that's been added—fawn—which I also slip into, going into people-pleasing mode and looking to the newest person to come along as my savior.) Typically, though, as my limbic system searches for the threat that causes my panic reaction and comes up empty, I start to shut down. I can almost imagine what it must be like to be in a coma—simultaneously fighting for your life while also being unable to move or speak. But while my body feels stuck, putting the words down on paper has freed part of my brain. Telling my story, going back through the events with a clearer head and a broader perspective, has also given me more compassion for myself.

It hasn't convinced me that I did everything perfectly—quite the opposite. But it's not about being right or wrong. This isn't a redemption story, because I shouldn't have to redeem myself. I am a multifaceted, nuanced person. Unfortunately, until now my story hasn't been told that way. There's not a lot of grace for imperfect survivors.

There were things I didn't foresee, moves that showed how foreign this all was to me. Of *course* there were. But shouldn't I have been guided through a formal, or at the very least organized, process by the people who knew the system?

I didn't fail to navigate the process. There never has been one.

I never thought of myself as a survivor, a whistleblower, or an activist before the events in 2018. Those roles carry too much weight, the expectation of perfection. What I'm finally coming to understand is that being imperfect doesn't disqualify you from speaking out, finding peace, and healing.

THROUGH WRITING THIS book, I've gotten clarity on the question "What made you come forward?" But the question that's much harder to answer is "What happened afterward?"

I wanted this book to set the record straight, but if I'm being perfectly honest, I was also kind of bitter that I was the one who had to do it. There were all these brilliant politicians, lawyers, publicists, activists, and journalists around me, but I was ultimately the one who had to paddle back out and fix it.

I might have been resentful, but in some ways, I understand why it must be me. I can offer insight to all the other people who might not have chosen this path for themselves either but who have chosen to do what's right in the face of a seemingly all-powerful opposition, a monster of a wave. I've learned that sometimes you don't do it because you are a natural-born disrupter. You do it because you have the power to help push the tides in the right direction. To cause a ripple that might one day become a wave.

I read a book back in grad school called *The Structure of Scientific Revolutions*. It describes how science has evolved through breakthroughs and new waves in technology, research, and theory that are unseeable at the time and are only recognized in retrospect.

That's the thing about revolutions—you typically can't see them while they're happening. They're usually met with more suspicion than belief. And they're only really solidified and celebrated in hindsight.

Maybe it's the scientist in me, but I'd like to believe that we're in the middle of a revolution that will only be recognizable in years to come. If it takes countless survivors to tell their story despite personal risks and consequences on an individual level—all of us slowly stacking on top of one another until there is finally a collective response—I'm proud to have contributed. If my act of speaking out plays a role in an eventual paradigm shift, ending stigma around sexual assault and holding powerful people accountable for their actions, then I accept whatever personal sacrifices I had to make.

THE FIRST TIME I tried to get my story down, a few years ago, I was so deep in the abyss of smear campaigns and security risks that it came across as saying, "Hey, everyone else who might be down in a similar hole, stay there. Don't even try to come out."

I stepped away, focused on getting better. But I came back to it, determined to tell my story so the world can know the scale of the problem and so we can work to make sure that future generations understand that when one person steps forward to speak truth to power, it does more than just redeem them or atone for wrongdoing. It adds to a collective whole, a larger wave of fresh outrage and demands for our government, our representatives, and everyone to not just #BelieveWomen but to *do better*.

Every swell starts with one wave. The world changes when the regular, imperfect people who have been on the beach look out at what's happening—fear and uncertainty hurling at them with unstoppable force—and decide to paddle out and take their chances. When enough of us do it, justice will finally prevail.

See you in the water.

Love,
Christine

ACKNOWLEDGMENTS

Thank you and love to the letter writers across fifty states and forty-two countries. You provide a continuous source of support and have inspired this book and several scientific research projects on sexual violence. I hope to figure out a way that we can connect.

To the love of my life, Russell: You are the everything (R.E.M.). To our kind and resilient sons, thank you for being you during the long storm. We love you googol.

Thank you for keeping us safe: Ron Conway and family, Santa Cruz Police, Dennis Burns, Execushield, Joshua, Gavin de Becker Associates, Bower Associates, Jay Collier & Associates, Redwood Security, Palo Alto Police, Chief Andy Mills, architect Mona Reeves, Stanford School of Medicine and Palo Alto University security, and all of our incredible neighbors.

A very special thank-you to the family who lent us their house and inspired us to pay that forward.

Thank you to my parents, the world's greatest grandparents. Thank you for introducing me to the Ocean, showing me love and patriotism, and providing the education that allowed me the privilege to speak up and to endure difficult times.

Thank you to those who made this book happen. Thank you, Emma Parry, for four years of advocacy and friendship. Thank you Jennifer Enderlin, Elisabeth Dyssegaard, Elisa Rivlin, Tracey Guest, Laura Clark, and the entire talented team at St. Martin's Press for your support and patience. Immense gratitude to Hilary Swanson—there will forever be a lounge chair saved for you. Thank you, Domenica Alioto, for your initial spark.

Thank you to inspiring books and their authors: Charles Nordhoff and James Norman Hall, *Mutiny on the Bounty*; Homer, *The Odyssey*; Jackie Speier, *Undaunted*; Glennon Doyle, *Untamed*; Amanda Gorman, *Call Us What We Carry*; Adam Frankel, *The Survivors*; Anita Hill, *Believing*; Chanel Miller, *Know My Name*; Andrew McCabe, *The Threat*; Valerie Jarrett, *Finding My Voice*; Tarana Burke, *Unbound*; Mazie Hirono, *Heart of Fire*; Siddhartha Mukherjee, *The Emperor of All Maladies*; and Gerry Lopez, *Surf Is Where You Find It*.

Love and gratitude to Deborah Katz and Lisa Banks— thank you for your fierce advocacy. Thanks to all who provided exceptional counsel and guidance: Larry Robbins, Michael Bromwich, Ricki Seidman, Barry Coburn, Bryan Thompson, Joe Cotchett, Nathan Ballard, Kendra, Melissa, Molly, Leah Nelson, Katie Gommel, Penelope Hoops, and Jeanie Newman.

Thank you to the many women role models and others who shared strength, wisdom, and kindness: Jackie Speier, Dr. Sally Hays, Dr. Maureen O'Connor, Amanda Gorman, Amanda de Cadenet, Mazie Hirono, Anita Hill, Cindi Leive, Valerie Jarrett, Oprah Winfrey, Anna Eshoo, Heidi Heitkamp,

Chanel Miller, Kamala Harris, Nancy Pelosi, Laura Blasey, Stacey Rubin, Dr. Katherine Stovel, Laurene Powell Jobs, Dr. Helena Kraemer, Ashley Judd, Gwyneth Paltrow, Tracy Powell, Aly Raisman, Lisa Erspamer, Dr. Booil Jo, Dr. Jennifer Freyd, Dr. Whitney Colella, Deb Ramirez, Dr. Vanessa Tyson, Dr. Gayla Margolin, Dr. Karen Gallagher, Shannon Brayton, Gloria Steinem, Dr. Estelle Friedman, Bridgit Mendler, Rowena Chiu, Karen Chapman, Rachel Denhollander, Dahlia Lithwick, Danielle Levitt, Sophia Sartain, Ruth Guthery, Sandy Mendler, Dr. Deb Peters, Haley Peters, Jackie Clement, Lisa Blasey, Andrea Bueno, my students and colleagues at PAU and Stanford Psychiatry, and the 2020 Stanford CASBS Fellows class.

Thank you to our team of letter openers and readers for your love and care of the letter writers, ensuring they were heard: Lizzy Michaels; Tess Brown; Emily Felber; Mikaela Bean; Aiden Cowie; Diego Mazzon; Jean Kavanagh; Aine O; Rachel Knauss; Fi, Bella, and Allie; and Danielle.

Thank you all friends old and new. To our community, who kept our locations quiet; sent us home-cooked meals or Popeyes chicken; drove kids to school; signed up for activities and classes by deadlines; asked their kids to check in; kept our pets; donated money for our security detail; checked on our house; collected the mail; sent heart emoji texts, loving notes, and videos of the world outside; attended the vigil; braved the media; endured retaliations; answered middle-of-the-night phone calls; checked on our well-being; allowed us time and space; hung out on a lounge chair; threw footballs to kids on the diving board; restrained from sending me news articles; tried to distract us; or listened for hours. It all helped more than I can ever describe. You never know who will help in life's toughest times. An incalculable thank you to Sam and Samu and other high school friends who showed up in different ways. We are forever grateful to the entire Palo Alto community and to so many who helped us survive. Thank you and love: Kirsten, Jim G, Sierra, Mercedes, Ana, Agustina, Carissa, Adrienne, Elizabeth and Stephanie, Tanya, Lissa, Diana, Lindsay, Chris, Mikka, Adela, Deepa, Dinraj, Jean, Keith, Jay, Kate, Dan, Catherine, Allison, Tina, Beth, Bruce, Nancy, Alan, Tommy F, Tommy S, Doug, Joe, Rachael, Danielle, Jeff, Klara, Matt, Sara, Erin, Kimberly, Shashank, and George.

Thank you to organizations and spaces that elevate discovery and kindness: Santa Cruz State Junior Lifeguards, California State Parks, Rio Del Mar Beach, JLS Middle School and Gunn High School, Palo Alto University, Pepperdine University, Stanford University School of Medicine, UCSC Seymour Marine Discovery Center, University of Southern California, Emerson Collective, CASA, Futures Without Violence, National Women's Law Center, March for Our Lives, Change the Ref, RAINN, YWCA Silicon Valley, Boys & Girls Clubs of the Peninsula, ACLU SoCal, AAUP, American Psychological Foundation, Association for Women in Psychology, Godfrey Dadich, University Club of Palo Alto, Mourad of San Francisco, Stanford Center CASBS, The Clayman Institute, Tales of an Educated Debutante, The Marine Detective, KOPA Hoops, Palo Alto Midnight, Stanford Soccer Club, Tropic Seas, and Mike's Café.

Thank you to music that heals: Metallica, Soundgarden, TOTD, GnR, Pearl Jam, and Alice In Chains.

Thank you to the Ocean.